HOW TO CUSS IN WESTERN

ALSO BY MICHAEL P. BRANCH

Raising Wild: Dispatches from a Home in the Wilderness

Rants from the Hill: On Packrats, Bobcats, Wildfires, Curmudgeons, a Drunken Mary Kay Lady, and Other Encounters with the Wild in the High Desert

PRAISE FOR *RAISING WILD*

"This book is not exactly about wild landscapes but the life of a house-holding family placed out there with two verge-of-puberty daughters. It is about our daily reality, not our fantasy possibilities, and who knows today what these girls will have to say later? So it is remarkably interesting, lively, nontheoretical, and hopeful. The wild might be wildfire or bushy-tailed woodrats under the floor—not just to live with but to know them. Michael Branch's book points forward, not back."—GARY SNYDER

"At last! A home for Michael Branch's joyous dispatches from the high desert, which I have long followed with delight. If you're unfamiliar with Branch, prepare for your first encounter with a singular sensibility, bracing yet affable. In part a memoir of building a unique home in an extraordinary place, in part a treatise on cultivating, protecting, and loving the wild, and each other therein, *Raising Wild* is a wholly defiant, tender book bristling with spirit, intelligence, and mountains of laughs."—CLAIRE VAYE WATKINS, author of *Battleborn* and *Gold Fame Citrus*

"Michael Branch has been an essential figure in western letters for years. Now, in his marvelous *Raising Wild*, he brings us an intimate look at one remarkable family's lucky life situated more deeply into their place than most will ever know. Hugely loving but ardently unsentimental, open and curious yet skeptical as desert dust, Mike's dispatches shimmer. They mean so much, I could enjoy reading them even upside down, or back to front." —ROBERT MICHAEL PYLE, author of *Sky Time in Gray's River*

"Not since Rachel Carson's *Sense of Wonder* has there been such a lively and evocative account of intergenerational experiences in nature. Michael Branch's *Raising Wild* offers breathtaking lyricism, sage wisdom, and big belly laughs in equal measure. Most importantly, this collection is a testament to the value of marrying memory and place—especially while in the company of those we love."—KATHRYN MILES, author of *Superstorm*

"Reading Michael Branch's prose is like attending a great and raucous party. A party held around a campfire in a secret corner of the wilderness full of intense talk, laughs, liquor, and deep insights. That the kids are invited this time makes it even better. A profound and moving book that just might change some lives."—DAVID GESSNER, author of *All the Wild That Remains*

"I have long considered Michael Branch one of the true visionaries of western American literature—and here is further proof. This beautiful, often raucous account of fatherhood and (wild) faith takes us even deeper into his remarkable kinship with northwestern Nevada. A place where, through the 'daily practices of love, humility, and humor,' we can all learn to be at home in this world."—JOHN T. PRICE, author of *Daddy Long Legs*

PRAISE FOR *RANTS FROM THE HILL*

"Think: Cagney amid the cacti."—*Las Vegas Review-Journal*

"Lyrical and subversive, the book is a rollicking celebration of living a joyously untamed life. An engagingly quirky collection."—*Kirkus Reviews*

"There have been dozens of hermit-in-the-woods Walden-like memoirs and essay collections written since Henry David Thoreau's death, but few capture Thoreau's raw, stubborn love for the natural world with as much humor and honesty as Michael P. Branch's *Rants From the Hill*."—*Chicago Tribune*

"Branch's humorous storytelling offers both natural history and life lessons. Readers may not realize they are learning while smiling. . . . Branch communicates his love of family and the natural environment through both wit and seriousness."—*Whole Terrain*

HOW TO CUSS iN WESTERN

AND OTHER MISSIVES FROM THE HIGH DESERT

MICHAEL P. BRANCH

ROOST BOOKS

BOULDER // 2018

Roost Books
An imprint of Shambhala Publications, Inc.
4720 Walnut Street
Boulder, Colorado 80301
roostbooks.com

9 8 7 6 5 4 3 2 1

First Edition
Printed in the United States of America

♾This edition is printed on acid-free paper that meets the
American National Standards Institute z39.48 Standard.
♻This book is printed on 30% postconsumer recycled paper.
For more information please visit www.shambhala.com.
Distributed in the United States by Penguin Random House LLC
and in Canada by Random House of Canada Ltd

Library of Congress Cataloging-in-Publication Data
Names: Branch, Michael P., author.
Title: How to cuss in western: and other missives from the high desert /
Michael Branch.
Description: Boulder, Colorado: Roost Books, 2018.
Identifiers: LCCN 2017044337 | ISBN 9781611804614 (paperback)
Subjects: LCSH: Branch, Michael P.—Homes and haunts—Great Basin. | American
wit and humor. | Wilderness areas—Great Basin. | Parenting—Great Basin.
| Natural history—Great Basin. | Great Basin—Description and travel. |
Nevada—Description and travel. | BISAC: HUMOR / Form / Essays. | NATURE /
Essays. | BIOGRAPHY & AUTOBIOGRAPHY / Personal Memoirs.
Classification: LCC F789 .B725 2018 | DDC 979—dc23
LC record available at https://lccn.loc.gov/2017044337

For my wife, Eryn
without you no stories

Everything is held together with stories. That is all that is holding us together, stories and compassion.

—BARRY LOPEZ, *Winter Count* (1981)

———

However, a good laugh is a mighty good thing, and rather too scarce a good thing; the more's the pity. So, if any one man, in his own proper person, afford stuff for a good joke to anybody, let him not be backward, but let him cheerfully allow himself to spend and be spent in that way. And the man that has anything bountifully laughable about him, be sure there is more in that man than you perhaps think for.

—HERMAN MELVILLE, *Moby-Dick* (1851)

———

I hope to make pictures like I walk in the desert—under a spell, an instinct of motion, a kind of knowing that is essentially indirect and sideways. Of all the things I wondered about on this land, I wondered the hardest about the seduction of certain geographies that feel like home—not by story or blood but merely by their forms and colors. How our perceptions are our only internal map of the world, how there are places that claim you and places that warn you away. How you can fall in love with the light.

—ELLEN MELOY, *The Anthropology of Turquoise: Reflections on Desert, Sea, Stone, and Sky* (2002)

CONTENTS

LAUGHING MATTERS

I F YOU'RE FAMILIAR with my recent books *Raising Wild* and *Rants from the Hill*, you already know that I live with my wife and two young daughters at 6,000 feet on a windy, desiccated hilltop in the remote western Great Basin Desert of Nevada. It is a choice of home that has led some folks to question our sanity, but this extreme landscape suits us perfectly. Our passive solar home floats like a speck in a vast sagebrush ocean, while the immensity of land surrounding it—rocky hills, expansive playas, forking arroyos, imposing snow-capped peaks—inspires and humbles us daily. Here we are beset by blizzards, flash floods, earthquakes, drought, and wildfires, not to mention the mundane challenges of packrats living within our walls, rattlers shading on our porch, and scorpions hiding beneath, well, everything. It is not despite these challenges but rather because of them that we consider this the most captivating home imaginable.

In the fifteen years my family has been dug in here on Ranting Hill, we've come to appreciate that this landscape is more sublime than beautiful, that it still has the power to terrify us. The allure of this gorgeous place is closely related to the fact that it is such a difficult place to live in—an apparent contradiction that hints at the complicated relationship I have with my home desert. Big winds sweeping down from the Sierra have driven snow a yard deep on our half-mile-long driveway, trapping us on the hill for days. Flash floods have blasted through the open desert, cutting away the roadbed and rendering our home inaccessible. Three times we have been forced to evacuate as wind-driven wildfire scoured these desert hills, with the closest call occurring last summer when a curtain of flames came within thirty feet of our outbuildings before the Jackpot Fire was at last stopped using our dirt driveway as the final firebreak. This is no pastoral retreat but rather a place of direct encounter with the daunting forces of a vast, high-elevation desert. Where we live, the idea of human control over nature is an unsustainable fantasy that we simply can't afford to maintain. But in place of that dangerous fantasy, which the wider culture propagates at every turn, this landscape offers the far more redemptive insight that we are part of something much larger than ourselves. This is a simple intuition but one so wild and expansive as to thoroughly shape our shared life here on Ranting Hill.

Living in such a wild landscape has two opposite and equally profound effects: developing a deep love of place provides solace, but it also threatens despair. We consider our home desert the most spectacularly beautiful place on earth, but in our years on Ranting Hill the storms have become more intense, the droughts more severe, and the wildfires more frequent and dangerous. My family simply cannot ignore the all-too-real effects of climate change. Rather, the new normal of powerful storm, drought, and fire directly affects our safety and quality of life, as well as placing new strains on the health of our home ecosystem. In the larger world beyond Ranting Hill, global warming and biodiversity loss

Laughing Matters

are just two of the planetary-scale environmental crises that must now be faced. For those of us who care deeply about environmental protection, this is an especially trying time.

While no writer can offer readers an antidote to despair, *How to Cuss in Western* is my attempt to share with you three of the most sustaining and sanative influences in my life—positive forces that have buoyed me as I've bobbed along in the vastness of this sagebrush sea.

The first of these three nourishing influences is place itself. Soon after we moved to this remote desert, I set out on a mission: over the course of a single year, I would walk at least 1,000 miles within a ten-mile radius of our house. My rationale for the experiment was that structuring my ambles according to this arbitrary annual goal might help me to get the lay of a land so vast and open as to at first feel inhospitable. Over time, this pedestrian experiment in covering miles became a kind of walking meditation that I found indispensable, and so I have over the intervening years continued my annual "thousand-mile walk to home," as I called it in *Rants from the Hill*. The experience of walking my home desert day after day, in all weathers and all seasons, has become richer and more meaningful to me over the years, as I've developed an intimacy with the land that would have been impossible for me to cultivate by any other means. These daily walks have now become small parts of a single, longer walk: a casual, fifteen-year, 20,000-mile stroll around my wild neighborhood.

Over the course of the many years I have been taking this long walk, life has had its ups and downs. But I have found that my ritual hikes through this desert wilderness have provided a vital form of stability and peace, a ballast when I am buffeted by crosswinds, a safe space even beneath the relentless sun and amid the coiled rattlers. There is solace in the liberating realization that this landscape, which was here long before me, will be here long after me as well. The desert abides. In that humbling perspective is a wild consolation that has brought calm in times of tumult, quiet in moments of distortion and noise. And while my high desert home remains an alien landscape to anyone who has not spent time in the Great Basin, strong attachment to place can occur anywhere, so long as the relationship is mindfully cultivated. The *environment* is an abstraction we can study, value, and manage, but a *place* is something we can love. I hope you will find the insights in *How to Cuss in Western* portable to your own home landscape, wherever you may happen to live.

The second of the three main salutary influences on me is family. When my wife, Eryn, and I made the decision to move out to Ranting Hill, we did not yet have children and could not at that time have imagined the joys and challenges that raising kids in such a wild place would bring. I can now say without hesitation that sharing this unusual adventure with my daughters has been the most hopeful experience of my life. It isn't simply that my countless field excursions with Hannah and Caroline are exciting, fascinating, and pleasurable—that we explore together how this wild desert works and what critters make their home here—but also that I've learned so much from the girls about how to engage with the natural world. In *Raising Wild*, I shared my observation that dwelling in the high desert has a great deal in common with parenting, because both are daily practices of love that inspire self-examination and ultimately lead to meaningful personal growth.

While I resist superficial platitudes regarding the angelic wisdom of children, there is something about our girls' playful and spontaneous approach to their home desert that I have found encouraging and even liberating. We grown-ups, freighted by our troubled pasts and distracted by our uncertain futures, tend to miss the magnificent, fleeting landscape of the present. Even so emancipated a saunterer as Henry David Thoreau occasionally carried the burdens of town life with him into the woods, writing in his provocative essay "Walking" that "it sometimes happens that I cannot easily shake off the village." The spontaneity and instinctiveness of childhood imagination, by contrast, offers a more direct path into the visceral beauty of the natural world. Being with my family in this wild place is a reminder to me of the immense value of reinhabiting the present, of striving to discover what Thoreau's mentor Ralph Waldo Emerson described as "an original relation to the universe." And that, I suppose, is the alchemy of love.

The third restorative influence I share with you in *How to Cuss in Western* is humor. Edward Abbey, my patron saint, once advised his readers to "Be loyal to what you love, be true to the Earth, and fight your enemies with passion and laughter." Our challenging historical moment has already demonstrated the striking efficacy of political satire, and I believe that the sword of humor will be wielded with increasing force and effectiveness in our ongoing battle against not just environmental injustice but social, economic, and racial injustice as well.

This book, however, offers humor not as a sword but rather as a shield, as a small inoculation against the diseases of frustration and fatigue that are epidemic among those of us who lament the uncertain fate of the planet. Because we care so deeply for this world yet fear we may be forced to watch it burn—or melt—we find that our love for nature is never unalloyed but is instead a bittersweet affection shot through with grief. For those who believe, as I do, that the global environmental crisis is urgent, and that it requires a moral as well as a strategic response, it may be difficult to imagine what's funny about any of this. But it is my belief that humor, in its remarkable power and dynamism, can help us to preserve the resilience that ultimately enables our courage and creativity.

In addition to having positive emotional and psychological effects, laughing has physiological benefits: it raises the heart rate and pulmonary ventilation, increases brain activity and alertness, stimulates the production of endorphins from the ventromedial prefrontal cortex, reduces the perception of pain, and enhances relaxation. Comedy also nurtures empathy, because the appreciation of humor requires flexibility, acceptance, and often the capacity to forgive both oneself and others. And humor has the power to bring people together, helping us to reexamine and, if necessary, rebuild our shared values and sense of common purpose.

I am concerned that those of us who care deeply about the environment have begun to imprison ourselves—and, worse still, our audience—within a windowless cell of humorless sanctimony. We extoll the virtues of sustainability, yet, in the intensity of our pursuit of what we feel certain is right, we often fail to sustain each other or even ourselves. We valorize community, yet too often lash out from a position of wounded isolation that keeps us from the joy we might otherwise discover, both in nature and in each other. How long will readers continue to turn the pages of another brittle eco-tirade or tacitly agree to suffer the misery registered in writing that functions primarily as tombstone? *How to Cuss in Western* instead employs the comic mode in the hope that humor can introduce some playfulness and pleasure to environmentalism—without compromising the fierce moral seriousness of its aims.

The core insight of the sustainability revolution is that before making choices we should carefully consider whether our actions can be perpetuated over time without causing excessive harm to the natural environment. I suggest that we also apply this reasonable standard to ourselves and our work, asking whether our current approach to environmentalism can be sustained, or whether our relentless solemnity now threatens to become a liability to our cause. It is precisely because we *are* serious—because our task is so difficult and the stakes are so high—that we should recognize the value of humor in helping to sustain both the natural environment and one another.

During the Q&A session following a recent reading of my work, an audience member asked me what I see as my main objectives as a writer. My unscripted reply was that "I want to make readers laugh. And I want to make them think. But I'm happiest when I help them to do both at the same time." Reflecting on this spontaneous answer later that night, I added the following to my journal: "I also want to help readers think about laughing. And, in a perfect moment, I would also get them to laugh about thinking."

A sense of humor, like a sense of place, is challenging to define precisely (as the term *sense* suggests), but we should be suspicious of folks who lack it, because laughter is an indispensable mode of self-reflection. Humor, like love, is fundamental to our humanity. It allows us to understand ourselves in a new way, to bond with other people and with the more-than-human world, to embrace with genuine humility the natural forces over which we exert no control. Most important, laughing matters because we recognize in laughter something essentially restorative and uplifting. In focusing only on what has been wounded, we risk forfeiting this regenerative potential of laughter. Humor, by contrast, can be a surprisingly powerful agent of both resistance and resilience.

It is in this spirit of renewed resilience that I share with you the twenty-nine small stories that comprise *How to Cuss in Western*. I hope they will give you an entertaining glimpse of our unusual life in these high, dry wilds, and also that they may serve to remind you of the sound of your own laughter.

HOW TO CUSS iN WESTERN

FEW AND FAR BETWEEN

THAT WE ARE SO FEW and far between in this big, wide-open high desert profoundly conditions our modes of communication, which in turn increases our dependence upon each other even as it intensifies the isolation we have intentionally chosen in coming here to dwell. Our challenge is to affirm the bonds of community to have them ready in times of blizzard and fire, while simultaneously protecting each other's elaborate fantasies of radical independence. This is more difficult than it might sound, and it accounts for the ubiquity of discussions about the weather, without which my neighbors and I—there are only eight of us strung along this terrible, 2.3-mile road snaking through the sage and juniper hills—would have a rough time getting along. We are all isolatoes out here, distinguished primarily by our reclusiveness. Ironically, the only thing we all have in common is that we each retreated to this remote desert to get away from other people—a shared passion that lays a crooked but necessary foundation for mutual aid in times of trouble.

The dominant ethic on our road—and the key to preserving harmony in our remote little desert kingdom—is unflinching, stoical restraint. One of my neighbors will use his tractor to clear our ditches after a flash flood, but not if we embarrass him by talking about it, never mind if we were to insult him by offering money. Another will sometimes plow us out after a big snow, but never if we ask or expect him to. Above all, we adhere strictly to the cardinal rule that there is to be no discussion of anything outside the immediacy of our local circumstances: weather, animals, and plants are permitted; religion, politics, and economics are not. What each of us does to make a living in the distant city is vaguely understood and never spoken of. The fact that 97 percent of topics common to human social discourse are strictly off-limits obviously necessitates conversations that are delicate, resourceful, and extremely brief. And this is just how we like it.

This ethic of restrained communication may be seen in the greetings we offer each other as we drive along our road—greetings that are confined entirely and inflexibly to the wheel wave. That is, we lift one or more fingers off the steering wheel of our trucks as we roll by each other in the mud, dust, or snow. This is a rich and subtle form of communication, with a complex variety of nuanced, unwritten rules, but I'd summarize it this way: You lift only your pointer finger off the wheel for a routine "howdy" to a neighbor. Raising the pointer and middle fingers in the two-fingered salute is appropriate when greeting a pickup carrying kids or older people, but it is best to flash the fingers at an oblique angle to avoid having the signal be misunderstood as a peace sign—which, in a sideways sort of way, it is. Under no circumstances do you *ever* allow your palm to leave the wheel, which would be a greeting so effusive and emotional—so perfectly hysterical—that anyone foolish enough to display such a loss of self-control would never regain the respect of their neighbors.

The complex, invisible protocol for wheel waving constitutes

HOW TO CUSS IN WESTERN

an interactive social symbol system that, like other kinds of coded language, appears inscrutable to outsiders but is highly functional for those of us who employ it. In a world replete with ambiguity, miscommunication, obfuscation, and deceit, this system is crystalline in its clarity, elegant in its simplicity and directness. You might object that the desert, so dry, has made us dry as well, and you may wonder if the wheel wave is a human-scale gesture on the order of the more demonstrative greetings that are regularly exchanged in town. And yet, in a high desert landscape that is so full of space, light, and wind, and so empty of confusion, misunderstanding, and noise, a sideways peace sign is sufficient—at least until the next blizzard or wildfire rolls in.

The unusual restraint that characterizes wheel waving may be related to the larger question of how we desert dwellers are influenced by the extraordinary land we inhabit. I am fascinated by the proposition that people who dwell in any physical environment long enough are inevitably and profoundly shaped by it. Out here in Silver Hills, we are buffeted by uncontrollable natural forces—from drought, wind, and blizzard to flash flood, earthquake, and wildfire. But we are also deeply affected by the crisp, thin air and the unique quality of the light, by the unforgiving openness of the land and the immense quiet it engenders. Even on a still day, a wind-canted juniper embodies the force of the Washoe Zephyr; even when it is desiccated, an arroyo is an expression of the sudden power of flood. In a similar sense, learning to live in the high desert might be described as the slow, humbling, graceful process of coming to realize how the high desert also lives in us.

I am certainly not the only writer to be fascinated by this question of environmental determinism in the arid West. Desolate as their reputation remains among folks who are looking for a handy place to test weapons of mass destruction or dispose of nuclear waste, American deserts have had as allies an impressive bunch of talented, passionate writers. Among these lyrical defenders I would include John C. Van Dyke, Joseph Wood Krutch, Wallace Stegner, Edward Abbey, Ellen Meloy, Charles Bowden, Ann Zwinger, Leslie Marmon Silko, Gary Nabhan, Terry Tempest Williams, and Craig Childs. And at the headwaters of this dry river of sparkling prose I would place Mary Austin, the early-twentieth-century writer who once described the arid West as "forsaken of most things but beauty and madness and death and God." We do not need to agree on what God might be to recognize how powerfully this expresses the exhilarating experience of desertness. In her 1903 classic *The Land of Little Rain*, Austin writes of the desert, "There are hints to be had here of the way in which a land forces new habits on its dwellers."

One of the habits forced on us by these expansive arid lands is a special kind of silence, one that mirrors the vast quiet of the landscape itself. Lately I've been thinking about this profound desert silence—how it might be shaping us even as we speak, or choose not to. I have observed that coyote and even raven talk more than we laconic Silver Hillbillies do. The few folks scattered along our rutted rural road seem to have agreed tacitly that language is a thing best left in town, and most of us ration words as we would a short supply of whiskey during a blizzard. Here in Silver Hills, we've reached a tacit agreement that the wheel wave is a sufficient expression of social connection.

To illustrate how this desert silence conditions our social interactions, I offer three small stories of unusual encounters with my rural neighbors.

The first occurred atop our home mountain, whose base is several miles west of our home on Ranting Hill and whose summit ridge runs north–south at a hair below 8,000 feet. To appreciate this story, you must first understand that, in fifteen years of walking these hills, canyons, and valleys—around 20,000 miles of tromping around my home desert in all seasons and all weathers—I have seen a grand total of three recreational hikers. When you run into another walker only every five years or so, you forget that such a meeting is even possible. Although I walk every single day, US presidential elections come and go more often than I encounter another desert rat like myself out in these inaccessible hills and canyons.

One bright morning in early fall, I had made the 1,800-foot ascent to the mountaintop and was picking my way south along the boulder-strewn crest of its summit ridge. As I came through a rocky notch in the ridge, I looked up and, to my great surprise, saw a man about 100 yards ahead, making his way toward me. I thought to myself how unlikely this meeting was and how much we two must have in common. Clearly, this was a guy I would want to talk with. On the other hand, I felt unsure about what I should say to him, since life here in Silver Hills has taught me deep respect for a kind of inviolable silence that now seemed oddly threatened by this chance meeting. We two came closer and closer to each other as we both walked carefully along the crest of the mountain, each of us glancing up occasionally at the other. At last, we came face-to-face on the narrow ridge. The guy looked at me and smiled.

"Hey," he said.

"Hey," I replied, returning the smile.

Neither of us broke stride.

The second encounter happened one October afternoon, as I was coming home from the Sierra with a load of white fir and ponderosa pine for winter fuel. I had just banked my pickup and dump trailer through the sharp double curve out on the paved road several miles east of Ranting Hill when I decided to pull over and check the load before starting up the washboarded gravel road to our house. As I tested the tension on the straps that secured the logs, I heard a vehicle enter the double curve, and I could tell from the gunning engine and squealing tires that the driver was taking the upper hairpin too fast. I looked up to see a pickup blast out of the top curve, leaning dangerously on its shocks and fishtailing. The driver managed to straighten it out, but the wobbling caused two boxes to fly off the full load in the truck's open bed. The first box turned out to be a cooler, which I discovered when it hit the asphalt, exploded into pieces, and sent a shower of beer cans skidding toward me. The other box was a plastic pet carrier, which bounced a few times before sliding across the road and coming to rest a few yards from the toe of my left boot.

The truck shuddered to a stop and out climbed a stocky guy wearing brown Carhartt pants, a Nevada-blue T-shirt, and a yellow tractor cap. He slalomed toward me, gathering the beer cans into his T-shirt, which he used as an improvised brew hammock. By the time he reached me, he must have had eight beers cradled in his shirt, and his belly, which was impressively hairy, was folded over the pewter oval of his big belt buckle. He reached casually into his suds pouch, pulled out a can of a local brew I recognized as Great Basin Outlaw Milk Stout, and handed it to me with a grin.

"Here," he said cheerfully, as if to apologize for nearly clobbering me with flying beers and pets.

"Thanks," I replied, accepting the badly dented can. With a friendly nod, he leaned over and grasped the pet carrier through its air holes with his thumb and middle finger, as if he were hoisting a six-pack. Walking back to his truck, he tossed the beers and pet box into the cab and sped away. I assume the pet carrier was empty, but I can't say so for sure.

The third encounter occurred on a breezy, snowless day in early November. I was walking along a dirt road in an open valley about five miles from Ranting Hill when I noticed the high-pitched drone of a small prop-engine plane above me. This was not unusual, since it is only about three miles from there to our local airstrip, which is used mostly to stage firefighting efforts along this stretch of the Sierra front. Soon, however, I heard the plane's engine surge and then cut out. After a few seconds of noiseless gliding, the engine fired again, but a moment later resumed missing, and then I noticed that the aircraft was losing altitude. Tracing a wide, descending circle above the valley floor, the plane banked behind me, the drone of its sputtering engine irregularly interrupted by moments of eerie silence.

I continued to walk, but now I found myself speeding up, looking over one shoulder and then the other at the plane's surprising descent. At last, it became clear that the pilot intended to use this dirt road as an emergency landing strip, and so I broke into a run, crashing off into the rabbitbrush to get as far away from the roadbed as I could. The next moment, the plane dropped over me and touched down gracefully in the middle of the road, pulling swirling clouds of amber dust behind it. It coasted to a stop, the door flew open, and a skinny man wearing a cowboy hat jumped out. Instead of coming toward me, though, he marched straight out into the open desert, heading in the general direction of the distant airstrip.

"Sorry!" he hollered at me over his shoulder, as he waded into the hip-deep sage.

"No problem, buddy!" I yelled back, as in the same instant I already regretted the terrible wordiness of my reply.

What is it about this desert that causes us to greet each other without lifting our palms from the steering wheel? How is it that, in a world brimming over with interminable chatter and incessant social media, we Silver Hillbillies became so laconic? Maybe we worry that spouting words might leave us desiccated and vulnerable to dehydration, or that the act of speaking might cause us to shed layers that provide a defense against hypothermia. Or is there simply so much space between us that we surprise each other when we meet and are struck with an aphasia induced by the vastness of the landscape itself? Or, perhaps we hesitate to speak because everything we say must be shouted into the desert wind, which sweeps our words away to Utah or, when the Washoe Zephyr quarters from the southwest, to Idaho. So, we clench our teeth to avoid eating dust and also for a more practical reason: to hold our souls in good and tight.

I think Mary Austin was right. Dwelling in the arid West has made us like the desert flowers, which have lived long enough in this hot wind to have learned the silent value of keeping a low profile.

WALKING TO CALIFORNIA

I F YOU HAVE EVER DRIVEN up Interstate 5 through northern California and into southern Oregon, you may have seen
the memorable bumper sticker that Oregonians use to welcome
their California neighbors over the state line: "Welcome to Oregon: Now Go Home." In rural Nevada, our view of Californians
is, if anything, less hospitable than that of our neighbors in Oregon. Out here in Silver Hills it can be dangerous to have California tags on your truck, and standard-issue summer attire in these
parts is a Nevada-blue T-shirt (with the sleeves cut off) featuring
the iconic shape of our state and emblazoned with the slogan, "I
Don't Give a Shit How You Did It in California." My neighbors
here in Silver Hills are about as likely to say something nice about
Californians as they are to drive to town and spend their whiskey
money to see a performance of *The Vagina Monologues*.

My own allegiances are more complex. As a Silver Hillbilly, I
too must publicly adopt a dismissive attitude toward Leftcoasters,
for without an affirmation of this shared disdain there are certain

neighbors with whom I would have absolutely nothing in common. My problem is that eighteen years ago, before I fully understood the consequences of my actions, I married a Californian. When Eryn asked me last year what I wanted as an anniversary gift, I requested simply that she quit admitting to our neighbors that she was born on the wrong side of the Sierra Nevada. I did not get my wish, but she did give me a travel guitar, which I now use to croon our state anthem, "Home Means Nevada," each time we head westward over Donner summit and begin the long descent into the Evil Empire.

I think *empire* is precisely the issue. Why do we western Nevadans deplore our neighbors from the nearby Golden State? Because we exist as a far-flung colony of their economic and cultural empire. It is their prosperity that is generated by provisioning our benighted colony with their vegetables and movies, smart phones and wine. And if it is they who Californicate our landscape with obscene McMansions built where sage grouse once strutted, it is also they who fuel our construction industry, bankroll our enterprise, and pull our slot handles. Because we rural western Nevadans have staked our identity on our fierce independence, we are secretly resentful of our economic reliance upon Californians, in precisely the same way people who live in resort towns want desperately for tourists to visit—and then proceed to despise them from the moment they arrive. This may also explain why so many Nevadans demonstrate a fierce antipathy toward the federal government. Such hostility obscures the awkward truth that without the substantial mining, ranching, and military subsidies we receive from Uncle Sam, quite a few of us would be out of business. And if that happened, we might have to move—to California.

My personal relationship to the Golden State is complicated by this additional fact: I walk to California now and then. Living at 6,000 feet in the extreme western Great Basin Desert means that California looms on our sunset horizon. Westward from our home the sagebrush ocean ripples out in a series of lovely, undulating foothills, then a sweeping, windy trough of valley, above which crests the ridge of our 8,000-foot home mountain. One of the many interesting things hidden among the mountain's wildflower-strewn summit meadows and shattered granite palisades is the Nevada-California state boundary. From our home on Ranting Hill it is a walk of several hours to reach the mountain's base, and then an 1,800-foot climb to gain its ridge. Once atop the mountain's spine, something curious and wonderful occurs. A view homeward, to the east, reveals the infinite sea of dust-green sage, crumbling sandstone palisades, and expansive alkali flats that comprise the unmistakable skin of the Great Basin; but a view to the west features the exfoliating granite turrets and thickly carpeted conifer forests that bespeak the magnificence of the Sierra Nevada. It is an odd feeling to straddle the saddle summit of my Janus-faced home range, contemplating by turns the very different worlds it at once connects and separates.

The flora and fauna atop the ridge also reveal the mountain's complexity, its rich hybridity and ecotonality. On the same slope, you will find desert tree species such as Utah juniper growing alongside mountain species like Jeffrey pine. The wildflowers, too, offer a wild combination of the Great Basin and Sierra Nevada, with desert buckwheat and tower butterweed growing together in a sweeping summit valley where balsamroot and mule's ears also mingle, and even columbine may be found hiding in the dappled shade of coyote willow and trembling aspen. Most of our desert birds are here—raven, magpie, harrier, golden eagle, meadowlark, pinyon jay—but they share the mountain with western outliers such as the spotted towhee. This ridge is the annual highpoint for pronghorn antelope, which prefer the drier, lower valleys but also use the mountain's springs, near which, during autumn, pronghorn bucks hide their harems of does in the rocky niches of the summit valleys. Yet this is also where our largest herd of mule deer crosses while moving in the opposite direction each fall, the animals clambering from Sierra blizzard country down into the dry valleys, where they can nibble bitterbrush and avoid becoming snowbound prey of the mountain lions that frequent this range. And while this mountain and its Sierra deer do keep cougars in the area, it is also a place where I once tracked a black bear—an animal so alien to the desert that it must have snuffled the rabbitbrush and sage and turned for the sunset again.

In a gridded world that is incised by arbitrary yet often limiting artificial boundaries, our home mountain represents a real and meaningful boundary, for its backbone is the far-eastern or far-western frontier for many species that simply cannot endure a life that is any higher or lower, colder or hotter, wetter or drier. My home mountain is like a nameless saloon at the end of a long, dusty road in the remote outback of the Intermountain West: a place where all manner of desert rats wash up for the simple reason that this is the last place to patch a tire or check a baseball score, to get that hot coffee or cold beer we've been thinking about for hundreds of dusty miles.

The unreal boundary separating Nevada from California is on the mountain, too, and though I may unknowingly crisscross this invisible line a dozen times during a long day's walk, I never sense it as I pass. If I pause to ruminate on this transparent border—and on the incendiary identity politics it ignites in the inhabited valleys below me—it is only to recognize the spectacular irrelevance of the distinction it attempts to signify.

TIRED OF CHICKENS

IN A LIVE RECORDING of his song "Canned Goods," the American folk musician and hillbilly existentialist Greg Brown offers some midsong patter commenting on Pablo Neruda's wonderful poem "A Certain Weariness" ("Cierto Cansancio"), in which Neruda memorably wrote:

> I'm tired of chickens—
> we never know what they think,
> and they look at us with dry eyes
> as though we were unimportant.

Brown first paraphrases these lines and then adds, "It's true . . . they do . . . and we are. But it's hard to take that from a damned chicken." I can't help but agree that I would rather be looking into the starry night sky than into the hollow eyes of a hen when I experience the profoundly ennobling epiphany of my own cosmic insignificance.

And yet I, too, have become a keeper of chickens. I should confess that I find the growing popularity of chicken keeping a yuppie fad that I am not entirely comfortable being associated with. I am certainly no yuppie: I am not young, I am as far from being urban as I can manage without moving to Alaska, and I am professional only in the sense intended by Hunter S. Thompson, when he offered the shrewd observation that, "When the going gets weird, the weird turn pro." (This, in fact, is the insight that inspired my career as a professional writer.)

Like many of my follies, this keeping of hens is the fault of my young daughters, who were sure that raising chickens would be fun, because "they're so fluffy and yellow and *cute*." As a father, I have discovered that invocation of the four-letter word *cute* is usually a signal that trouble is brewing. I explained to Hannah and Caroline that the fuzzy-yellow, springtime stage of a chicken's existence lasts about forty-five minutes and is soon followed by protracted cohabitation with a feathered beast so vicious and scaly that keeping one is akin to having a pet baby dinosaur.

"Baby dinosaur?" exclaimed Caroline, "That's *epic*!"

All fathers of daughters come to learn the futility of resistance to anything deemed *cute*. So, in early May, we made the momentous trip to the feed store, where the girls chose four yellow fluff balls, whose best quality, I thought, was how incredibly cheap they were. But we also had to buy a big plastic tub to keep them in, plus a screen to cover the tub, a bag of shavings and some chick feed, a little water bin, and a spendy clamp-on heat lamp. The total cost of this outing was something like ten bucks for the chickens and another hundred to accessorize them, a thing-to-its-stuff ratio disturbingly reminiscent of Barbie dolls—another *cute* purchase that had left a sizeable dent in my hip.

We brought the baby birds home and set them up in the garage out of reach of our old dog, Darcy, and the girls had fun playing with them. Hannah named one "Henrietta," which was as sweet as it was inevitable, while Caroline insisted on "Eggcellent Chicken" for another. Eryn named the third chick "Susan Henimore Cooper" after the novelist James Fenimore Cooper's daughter, Susan, who wrote *Rural Hours*, the 1850 paean to the virtues of country living. I dubbed fluff ball #4 "D. B. Cooperetta," in honor of the aerial outlaw and American folk hero D. B. Cooper, who in 1971 hijacked a Boeing 727, extorted the airline for cash, and then parachuted out into the rainy darkness somewhere over the Pacific Northwest, never to be seen again.

Despite their cuteness and their clever names, the little chicks had pretty active business ends, and it inevitably fell to me to clean out what quickly became a bucket of dust, shavings, and fowl turds. The birds grew so quickly that it soon became necessary to acquire a coop and attached run, which I scored for two hundred dollars from an old man hawking them out of the back of his battered pickup in the parking lot of the only gas station in our valley. When the chicks grew large enough, we transferred them to their new home, which now required yet more shavings and an even larger water dispenser, not to mention a ridiculous amount of feed that the baby pterodactyls soon began to gobble up. There went another hundred bucks. Within forty-eight hours the coop and run were invaded by ground squirrels, which necessitated lining the entire bottom of the run with plywood and reinforcing the poultry netting around the whole operation, at a total cost of another C-note. When the first frost fell in autumn, I also had to add a device to prevent the birds' water from freezing; this, along with the heat lamp, required a heavy-duty extension cord, power strip, and timer.

After a few months, I had done a whole lot of coop cleaning, and we still had not a single egg. It was time to reckon the damage. Over a tumbler of sour mash, I determined that, although I was only out a ten-spot on the birds, everything they had needed to stay warm, healthy, hydrated, and out of the intestines of coyotes had run me a staggering seven hundred bucks. At fourish bucks a dozen for free-range eggs at the supermarket in town, the seven Benjamins I had shelled out on Susan Henimore and her chick quartet would buy more than two thousand eggs. I then calculated the likely lifespan and laying productivity of these squawking featherballs and determined that, even if a bobcat didn't eat them, these ladies could never squat them out at a rate that could approach the break-even point.

Then there are the chickens themselves, which attract coyotes and constantly require feed, water, and fresh shavings. There is nothing like coming home from a long day of work, pouring a few fingers of glowing hooch, parking my keister on the hearth in front of the woodstove, and then remembering that I have to pull on my snow boots and tramp out into the freezing wind to serve the chickens. It takes all the paternal sympathy I can muster not to "accidentally" leave the coop door open—a simple mistake that would allow Old Man Coyote to quickly solve a problem forced upon me by my daughters.

Worse still is the psychological trauma induced by looking at those small monsters, with their weird, bulbous heads and their scaly legs and scrabbly claws, their vicious beaks clacking as they squawk and strut around mindlessly. Those terrible eyes—so beady, shifty, devious. Dark pinpricks of nothingness! Is it any wonder people have so long questioned the motives of chickens crossing roads? Like Neruda, I'm tired of chickens. Like Greg Brown, I suspect that if there is any message concealed within their empty eyes, it has something to do with the Sisyphean insignificance of our own existence. Yet somehow, even while scraping up frozen chicken shit in ten-degree weather, that insight still strikes me as funny—even useful.

Although the hens at last began to lay a few eggs, they are still a reminder of why I am destined to remain a land-poor rural hobby farmer whose quest for pastoral bliss, if reckoned by the dollar, amounts to little more than an elaborately maintained affectation. I was reminded of how my own mother had once demonstrated the poor returns on a fishing trip I had taken with my dad by calculating the price-per-pound of the few fish we caught relative to the considerable sum we had spent to try our luck. But we were not buying fish, of course. We were buying an experience together, which Mom knew perfectly well. I am not in the chicken game to produce eggs. I am buying a shared experience with my daughters, and I consider that a fair deal, even if it comes at a high price.

The eggs we buy at the store are eaten, and nothing more. What does not end up in the septic tank may lodge in our cells, but there is no other payoff from the experience, no sense in which that store-bought egg will also lodge in our memory and imagination. But the small, beautiful, pointed, bluish egg left by Eggcellent Chicken is a different thing entirely. That is the product of something more than a chicken, purchased with something more than money, and enjoyed with something more than the need to chow down and race to town. When the girls crunch out through the snow to harvest that bluish gem—talking all the while to the birds, who also talk back to them—they are being nourished in some way that will not be reckoned by the dozen. Living up here on Ranting Hill will never pay, but I consider it a bargain just the same.

THE LEPRECHAUN TRAP

I T ALL STARTED when I made a small mistake on Mother's Day. It was an honest mistake, one anybody might have made. As a gift for my wife, Eryn, on her very first Mother's Day, I bought a garden gnome, which I presented to her along with a romantic expression of my love and appreciation. So complete was my naïveté at that time that I honestly believed I had done something wonderfully thoughtful. The gnome was not plastic but rather cast iron, a seventy-pounder the size of a small child that had to be moved with a hand truck and had set me back serious coin. This was not a gnome that said, "Hey, enjoy this until it breaks or we divorce, whichever comes first," but rather, "Honey, this gnome, like our love, is built to last."

Also in my defense, the weighty gnome was not standing, in that awkward lawn jockey pose into which so many gnomes are unhappily forced, but was fully supine, cradling a cork-topped bottle of hooch in the crook of his arm. He was sprawled out with feet crossed, reclining coolly on one elbow, with his head cocked, while his bearded face wore a mischievous, come-hither grin. In fact, the gnome looked kind of sexy, which seemed perfect. Having been married eighteen years, I now see the error of my ways, but I still maintain that the gnome, which to this day reclines, rusty and drunken, in the stippled shade of a bitterbrush bush, is a *quality* gnome.

For our young daughters, every year is a necklace strung with the sparkling beads of holidays—holidays I find both annoyingly frequent and often unforgivably obscure. For example, I am no longer happily ignorant of Hoodie Hoo Day, which is celebrated each February 20 by people who go outside precisely at noon, wave their hands over their heads like fools, and shout, "Hoodie-Hoo!" And how can I support Middle Name Pride Day on March 10? Can we not simply agree to be ashamed of our middle names, which should remain unspoken, except when parents chastise children for their abominable behavior? I see now that holidays were invented primarily for elementary school teachers, for whom the year would be impossibly tedious without them. In retaliation, I have begun insisting that my daughters help me to celebrate some obscure holidays that are more compatible with my own sensibility: Do a Grouch a Favor Day on February 16 (I receive rather than give), Defy Superstition Day on September 13 (my answer to evangelicalism), and Hermit Day on October 29 (which I desperately need to celebrate after having been subjected to so many ludicrous holidays throughout the year).

Recently we celebrated St. Patrick's Day, a holiday everyone in my family can get behind. While I am not entirely comfortable commemorating a guy who killed innocent snakes and talked pagans out of their perfectly serviceable native polytheism, I do recognize the solid common sense in appropriating religious holidays for the noble purpose of drinking whiskey. This year Caroline, having noticed the garden gnome, asked, "Is it a Leprechaun?" I explained that it was instead a *quality* gnome, adding that Leprechauns only sneak around on the night of March 17.

"Do they come all the way from Ireland?" she asked.

"Well, they're descended from Irish Leprechauns, who came to Nevada during the 1840s looking for a pot of gold," I replied. "They're all over the Great Basin now. Pretty much westernized, too—roper boots, big belt buckles, buckaroo Stetsons . . . green Stetsons."

"Does Old Man Coyote eat them?" asked little Caroline, who is obsessed with predation.

"Nope. Leprechaun is a trickster, like Old Man Coyote, so they just play tricks on each other." Now she frowned. "*But,*" I continued, trying for a quick recovery, "mountain lions *love* to gobble up Leprechauns."

Caroline flashed a wide grin. "Cool! I bet they crunch 'em right in their little necks and shake 'em hard!"

Big sister Hannah, whose credulity is matched only by her nerdiness, chimed in enthusiastically, "So, Leprechauns are invasive exotics!"

"Exactly," I said. "Just like your mother. Mommy came over the Sierra from California, trapped me, and then started having you mischievous little Nevada babies."

Hannah, who has seen me live-trap everything from field mice to ground squirrels, now asked, "Can we trap a Leprechaun?"

"No problem," I replied, "but you girls will have to help me build the trap."

The next week was incredibly fun. Hannah used graph paper to devise a floor plan for the Leprechaun trap, which we would construct from the cardboard box left over from the recent purchase of a shop vac. Like the native Nevadan she is, Hannah also insisted that we call the trap the Leprechaun Lounge, which, she observed astutely, sounded more welcoming. Hannah included in her architectural design a porch, which seemed a thoughtful addition to a trap. Caroline was also generous, suggesting that we add a potty. ("You know, Daddy, *just in case*," she whispered discreetly.) Each evening the girls added something new to the trap: a pile of gold coins, which they made by wrapping quarters in aluminum foil and coloring them with a yellow highlighter; a little doll's bed, in case the incarcerated sprite got drowsy; and, of course, green things, which are not easy to come by here in the high desert. Ultimately, the girls settled on a juniper twig, a small plastic dinosaur they call Braucus, and a cup full of mini-marshmallows soaked overnight in green food coloring.

At some point in our discussions of Leprechaunalia, I mentioned that the wee fellows are awfully fond of Irish whiskey, which prompted the girls to beg that I raid my liquor cabinet on their behalf. I soon discovered, however, that I had no Jameson or Old Bushmills, only fifteen-year-old Redbreast, a whiskey so fine and rare that I once declined to share it with my own mother, whom I love dearly. Yet here were these kids demanding that I put my liquid gold into a cardboard box while we snoozed away the night of March 17. Because their track record with cups of other liquids suggested that my *quality* hooch would end up watering the dust, I insisted upon being the one to place this delicious bait into the trap. Just before bedtime, we set up the Lounge just outside the slider door. Reluctantly, I poured a short glass of the precious Redbreast and carefully slid it into the Leprechaun trap while the girls looked on enthusiastically. We then nestled into our sleeping bags on the living room floor, where we began our stakeout of the trap.

After twenty minutes of vigilance both girls fell soundly asleep, and I got to thinking. The trap was cute, the girls were cute, the three of us snuggling in the mummy bags—all very cute. But now the girls were asleep, and my *quality* liquor remained in serious danger. The wind ripping down off the Sierra might upset the trap, and it was a cinch that field mice and kangaroo rats would scurry in and stick their whiskered snouts into that glass. Even evaporation—the beautifully named "angel's share"—seemed too cruel a fate for such *quality* booze.

At last I snuck out of my mummy bag, creeping on my hands and knees so as not to wake the girls. I eased the slider door open and crawled over the sill and out into the dirt, pausing momentarily to wonder if it was warm enough yet for scorpions to be out. Holding the Lounge's trap door open with one hand, I reached in slowly with the other, groping for the precious glass. But just as I did this I heard little Caroline behind me, like Cindy Lou Who: "Daddy, what are you doing out there?"

"Just checking the trap," I answered, as I stepped back inside and then snuggled her into her bag. "Nothing yet, honey."

Caroline was soon fast asleep once again, and I snuck back outside and finally retrieved the tumbler from the Leprechaun Lounge. Carrying the liquid bait that had attracted only me, I shuffled over to the rusty gnome and silently proposed a toast to St. Patrick. The gnome reclined, smiling broadly, as the night breeze whispered through the juniper and bitterbrush, and a spectacular conjunction of Venus and Jupiter illuminated the western sky.

If no little green men were captured that night, our imaginations certainly were. The girls, camping out near their homemade trap, woke to report that they were sure they had heard one of the sprites, and so they began immediately to adjust their design for next year's trap. For my part, I will always remember the *quality* moment in which, while standing watch nearby my slumbering daughters, the light of distant planets faintly illuminated the glowing elixir in that raised glass.

WILL THE REAL FAKE JOHN MUIR PLEASE STAND UP?

EVERY TIME Chautauqua season rolls around, I feel compelled to rant about this bizarre cultural practice, which Teddy Roosevelt once called "the most American thing in America"—never mind that this honor deserves instead to be shared by baseball, blues, and bourbon. Chautauqua is defined by its practitioners as "a public humanities educational event in which scholars portray historical characters." A more helpful definition was offered by little Caroline: "It's when grown-ups play dress-up and act like dead people they really like in a tent." It remains unclear to me why a form of education intended to be accessible to the entire community was given a name that even sober people cannot pronounce, much less spell. I am also troubled that Chautauqua is described as "living history," a term every bit as logical as "Congressional action," "industrial park," "clean coal," "adult male," "true story," and, in honor of this chapter, "act naturally."

I am uncomfortable with Civil War reenactors, department store Santas, and Chautauquans, all of whom I suspect of being not only impostors but also inebriates and pedophiles. That said, I agree with Chautauqua's core presumption, which is that anything is better than reading a history textbook. Given the choice between a scholarly tome and a lawn chair parked next to a cooler of IPAs, the decision to support Chautauqua is not so difficult after all. And if the concept is, as I understand it, to trick benighted Americans into learning something meaningful about our nation's past by seating us in the shade of a tent in a park and letting us drink beer, well then, I am all in.

My favorite thing about Chautauqua is that, like other entertaining spectator sports, it can go off the rails in a heartbeat. The source of this peril is the fact that folks in attendance at the event are permitted to ask questions of the performers, who are obliged to answer while remaining in character. I once saw a Chautauqua performance of Henry David Thoreau in which the would-be Transcendentalist was excoriated by an older woman for supposedly failing to do his own laundry. "Get a job, you bum!" she yelled at the hapless Thoreau impersonator. I've seen FDR interrogated about impeaching Donald Trump, Harriet Tubman asked what year the Underground Railroad to California was completed, Christopher Columbus exhorted to condemn the NFL team name "Redskins," and Mae West called out for her famous claim to have been Snow White before she drifted ("That just seems confusing," objected the earnest young woman from the audience). I have even seen Will Rogers verbally abused because of his "obviously entirely super false claim" to have never met a man he didn't like. (The inquisitor, in this case, was such a bloviating asshat that his behavior went a fair piece toward making his own argument persuasive.)

My buddy David Fenimore, who is the most gifted of the one Chautauquans ever to ascend Ranting Hill, has stories that last until the last bottle is empty. Once, while portraying the gold baron John Sutter, David's audience included a drunk guy dressed up like

HOW TO CUSS IN WESTERN

a Forty-Niner—a "One-Eyed, Snaggle-Toothed, Shaggy-Haired Hillbilly" who pulled a wagonload of pickaxes and gunny sacks behind him and shouted "Kick mah mule!" throughout the performance. On another occasion, David was playing Woody Guthrie to an appreciative crowd when a lady in a wheelchair rolled herself up to the stage and began loudly accusing him of being "a damned Communist!" Imagine spending months studying every detail of a fascinating life—David preps his roles by memorizing one thousand 5 x 7-inch index cards with facts related to his character—and then being hollered at by a soused miner or an enraged libertarian. Now *that* is public humanities education in the New West.

In some instances, the folks doing the portraying are every bit as batty as those on the receiving end of the performance. David relates the story of a local eastern Sierra mountain man who was a self-appointed Chautauquateer. "During the week, he made these giant, crappy chainsaw sculptures of bears, but every Saturday he'd come to town wearing a leather do-rag and claim to be Benjamin Franklin," David explained. "He really looked like Franklin, too—long stockings down below, long gray hair up top, big forehead, round specs—only everything he said was pure anti-Federalist tirade. No more taxation of kites, that kind of thing. Sort of a Joe Chainsaw portraying Rush Limbaugh portraying Ben Franklin. You shoulda heard him when he got going on axing the Postal Service."

The approach of Chautauqua season always reminds me of a memorable run-in I once had with some fake John Muirs. Having some years ago written a book on Muir, I was making the lecture circuit, blathering Muiriana at anyone who would listen. At one point, I was booked at a conference of hard-core Muirites, where I shared the program with Lee Stetson, an experienced Chautauquan who had been commissioned to do his acclaimed performance of Muir that evening. Lee has been doing his fake Muir thing since about the time Muir died in 1914, and it is *honed*. He has quite simply out-Muired Muir. Lee looks like Muir, acts like Muir, and he's got Muir's mild Scottish brogue nailed. I would even believe Lee if he told me that he *smells* like Muir. And do not make the mistake I did, of pulling on his long gray beard, because his face foliage is as real as was Muir's own.

The trouble started that night at the party that was held after Lee's excellent Chautauqua performance of Muir. I was not selling many books, so I abandoned the signing table for the libations table, pitching camp next to a large tub of icy Sierra Nevada Pale Ale. After half an hour of elbow bending I noticed Lee across the room. He was wearing Muir's familiar, well-worn leather vest and signature weathered hat. A crook-handled Sierra cup dangled from his hand-tooled belt, and, though he faced away from me, I could just make out a bit of his flowing white beard. I crossed the room and tapped him on the shoulder to congratulate him on his performance. But when he turned I was surprised to discover that this was not the real fake Muir but rather was an interloping, fake fake Muir, a second-rate wannabe who apparently had his own John O'Mountains fetish.

"Who are you?" I asked.

"Waahl, Laddie, of caarse I'm none otherrr than Johnny Muirrr!" he shouted at me.

I cringed at his abominable brogue, which was closer to Mike Myers's portrayal of Fat Bastard in the Austin Powers movie franchise than to Sean Connery's portrayal of Agent 007 in the old James Bond flicks. His costume was somehow too Muiry, as if he were suited up to play the famous environmentalist during a spirted evening of trick-or-treating. Plus, this cartoonish Muir was unacceptably amped-up, as John Muir might have been had he lived in the era of the Venti Triple Cinnamon Dolce Crème Frappuccino. Needless to say, I beat a hasty retreat to the beer bucket.

Popping another ale, I glanced up and, once again, saw a fake Muir across the room. But this time I noted that the tan of his leather vest appeared darker, and his hat seemed to have a slightly different cut to it—though the snowy beard and Sierra cup flowed and dangled just as before. I surmised that this must be the authentic fake John Muir, and so I grabbed my ale, cracked a second one for him, and once again strode across the room, this time intending both to congratulate Lee on his performance and also to alert him to the presence of an impostor fake Muir. As before, I tapped him on the shoulder, but, when he turned, I discovered, to my dismay, that this was yet *another* fake fake Muir, disconcertingly different from both the real fake Muir and the first fake fake Muir, and considerably less convincing than either one.

I looked him dead in the eye and took a long slug of first one beer and then the other. "And who are *you*?" I asked.

"Why, matie, I be the man John Muir!" he exclaimed, with an enthusiasm every bit as cloying as that displayed by the first fake fake Muir.

But rather than featuring a thick brogue, this guy just sounded like he was doing a flaccid imitation of a pirate, and his costume was much worse than a Halloween get-up. He also wore heavy makeup, and I picked up a whiff of what seemed to be pine-scented perfume. He looked like he was outfitted to play Muir in a burlesque show.

"OK, this won't do at all," I said. "Please go wait by the beer bucket, happy pirate. I'll be right back." I combed the room until I found the first fake fake Muir and asked that he, also, adjourn to the pale ale station. Then I hunted around until I located the real fake Muir, who was sitting calmly outside on the porch, chatting quietly with a friend.

"Lee, have you seen this shit?" I interrupted at first sight of him. "This place is crawling with fake Muirs, man. They look awful, and they sound worse. One of them even smells like cheap air freshener. We have to put a stop to this."

I thrust a beer his way. He thanked me, took a slow sip, and replied calmly that a proliferation of Muirs was surprisingly common. Speaking in the kindest tone imaginable, he explained that he not only tolerated but even provided friendly encouragement to these bogus fake Muirs wherever he might encounter them.

Lee's reply was so humane and compassionate that I paused momentarily before returning to my senses. "Nope, no, no, no, no, nope," I said. "Absolutely not. We are *not* going to encourage this kind of thing. This party isn't big enough for more than one fake Muir. Come with me."

I coaxed Lee up, and into the reception we went, where we found both of the fraudulent fake Muirs waiting, as instructed, by the ale tub. Then I whistled loudly to draw the attention of the sixty or so people at the party.

"It is intolerable to have three guys walking around acting like Muir," I declared. "We'll settle this hot mess right now. We're going to have a Muir-off. Side betting is allowed, but no assisting of any Muir will be permitted. The two losers must never again pretend to be a fake John Muir."

I popped open another brew and began peppering the men with questions. "In 1866, you saw your first piece of writing published. What was its title?" I asked.

"*A Glorrrious Saunterrr?*" guessed thick-brogued Muir.

"Be it *A Botanical Ramble?*" asked whitebeard, the pirate.

"*The Calypso Borealis*," answered Lee Stetson, gently.

"*Calypso Borealis* is correct," I said.

"In 1867, you set out on a walk that took you 1,000 miles from Indianapolis to the Gulf of Mexico," I continued. "But what was your original destination?"

"Florrrida!" yelled broguey fake Muir, enthusiastically.

"It be Cuba!" trumped pine-scented, burlesque fake Muir.

"The Amazon," said Lee in a mild voice.

"The Amazon is correct," I replied.

"And before you started on that journey, you were temporarily blinded when you accidentally struck yourself in the eye with what object?" I asked.

"A scrrrewdrrriverrr," replied Fat Bastardy fake Muir.

"It be a file," answered crappy pirate fake Muir.

"The *tang end* of a file," corrected Lee, modestly.

"The tang end of a file is correct," I confirmed. Switching my beer to my left hand in order to rest my right hand on Lee's shoulder, I announced the verdict. "I hereby declare victorious the only guy at this party who both stabbed himself in the eye with the tang end of a file and also knows what the hell the tang end of a file is. This, my friends, is the one-and-only true, original, authentic, genuine *real* fake John Muir."

There followed an enthusiastic round of applause. Lee smiled graciously, without a hint of condescension. "You there, Fat Bastard and Swashbuckling Crossdresser," I addressed the pair of impostor fakes, "relinquish your beards."

The two men sheepishly removed their fake beards—which weren't even glued on but, rather, were strapped to their faces with cheap elastic cords—and, with an air of genuine solemnity, laid them down on the table. I handed each of them a beer and gave each a consoling slap on the back, which triggered a second round of applause. The buccaneer Muir retreated honorably and soon after returned to the party dressed like an English professor. The broguey Muir became quite drunk, strapped his fake beard back on, and claimed to be the nature writer John Burroughs.

I realize that it is easier to rag on a Chautauquan than to be one, which is why I am a reclusive humor writer and not a public performer of "living history." But I am in sympathy with all those fake Muirs out there. And the counterfeit Thoreaus, Tubmans, and Twains, too, the impostor Jeffersons, Stowes, and Lincolns, and the imitation Communist Woody Guthries—even the do-ragged, chainsaw bear–sculpting libertarian Ben Franklins. Given that most of us spend a fair amount of energy pretending to be somebody we aren't, we might as well aim high. We could do worse than to emulate the real Muir, who kept the Wal-Marts out of Yosemite Valley. So, Johnny, here's a pint of Sierra Nevada in the air to the hope that we can all be a wee bittie more like you.

SUCH SWEET SORROW

ONE OF THE BEST reasons to celebrate Independence Day is that it reminds us to ask anew what it means to be truly independent. This question is especially important for Westerners, since our region has, for better and worse, been viewed as the nation's symbolic repository of freedom. In the American cultural imaginary, to head west has meant to journey into an unfettered land where individuality triumphs over social convention. Among the many signs of freedom and independence in the West, I'd count our intense individualism, the fierce beauty of our public lands, and our disdain for repressive social constraints. And no social constraint is more repressive than the widespread public prohibition against flatulence. That is why, as a celebration of independence, I offer this defense of the fart.

Question: what do Aristophanes, Seneca, Dante, Chaucer, Rabelais, Montaigne, Shakespeare, Jonson, Milton, Swift, Franklin, Melville, Twain, Joyce, Beckett, Auden, Salinger, and Roth have in common with Edward Abbey? Answer: they all wrote fart jokes.

By the time Aristophanes was cutting cheese jokes—jokes that involve none other than Socrates himself—in his wonderful play *The Clouds* in 423 BCE, flatulence humor had been around for fifteen hundred years. We now know that the oldest joke in recorded history is in fact a fart joke. After a three-month study of a Sumerian tablet that has been dated to 1900 BCE, a team of scholars emerged with this illuminating translation of the tablet's cuneiform text: "Something which has never occurred since time immemorial; a young woman did not fart in her husband's lap." I do not intend to argue that this joke is the apogee of tailwind humor, though it must have been a reliable gut-buster among the Sumerians if they judged it worthy of chiseling into stone for the sake of posterity. I want only to make this simple point: we've been writing fart jokes for at least four thousand years. And there's no telling how long backdoor breezes have been blowing in the humor of oral traditions from around the globe. And why has the lowly fart enjoyed such a long and distinguished cultural pedigree? Because unfettered farting has long been associated with freedom from societal constraint. Flatulence is forever wedded with humor because both are potent forms of attack on institutional authority and social conformity.

Classical literature is rich with flatulence humor. In Dante's *Divine Comedy*, the final line of *Inferno* chapter 21 reads: *ed elli avea del cul fatto trombetta*. Translation? "And he used his butt as a trumpet." In Chaucer's "The Miller's Tale," the poor student, Nicholas, blows a bean before the parish clerk, Absalom. (*Urban Dictionary* lists 261 synonyms for fart; I'm taking pains to include as many as I can here.) Chaucer writes that Nicholas "let fly a fart as loud as it had been a thunder-clap, and well-nigh blinded Absalom, poor chap." And it's easier to find a Shakespeare play that features a fart joke than to hunt up one that doesn't. Act 3 of *The Comedy of Errors* contains my favorite of these Elizabethan breeches burners: "A man may break a word with you, sir, and words are but wind; Ay, and break it in your face, so he break it not behind." In other words, better to break a promise than to break wind. In the *Arabian Nights'* "Tale of Abu Hassan" a man flees in embarrassment after letting rip a fog slicer during his own wedding. He returns from his self-imposed exile a decade later to discover that his vaporous transgression has become so famous that it is being used to date events in the recent history of the country. "Verily [my] fart has become a date!" the man exclaims proudly. "It shall be remembered forever!"

There has also been plenty of comic celebration of gas here in America. The greatest of American poot humorists is Benjamin Franklin, whose wonderful open letter "To the Royal Academy of Farting" (circa 1781) suggests that the discovery of a means to convert flatulence into something more pleasing would represent a monumental contribution of science to humanity. In *Moby-Dick*, Melville wastes no time getting to the fart jokes in the novel's opening chapter, where Ishmael explains: "I always go to sea as a common sailor, because of the wholesome exercise and pure air of the forecastle deck. For as in this world, head winds are far more prevalent than winds from astern (that is, if you never violate the Pythagorean maxim)." Ishmael here refers not to the Pythagorean *theorem* you vaguely remember from eighth-grade math class but rather to the Pythagorean *maxim*, which is the injunction to avoid eating beans because they tend to fire up the trouser trumpet.

It is exactly this Pythagorean flatulaphobia that Edward Abbey, that most outspoken of environmental humorists, denounces in the work of his literary forefather, Henry David Thoreau. In "Down the River with Henry Thoreau," Cactus Ed first describes his own breakfast, then pivots to an incisive critique of Thoreau's take on food and farting:

Scrambled eggs, bacon, green chiles for breakfast, with hot *salsa,* toasted tortillas, and leftover baked potatoes sliced and fried. A gallon or two of coffee, tea and—for me—the usual breakfast beer. Henry would not have approved of this gourmandising. To hell with him. I do not approve of his fastidious puritanism.... Thoreau recommends a diet of raw fruits and vegetables; like a Pythagorean, he finds even beans impure, since the flatulence that beans induce disturbs his more ethereal meditations. (He would not agree with most men that "farting is such sweet sorrow.")

In referencing flatulence in this comic send-up of a romantic line from Shakespeare's *Romeo and Juliet,* Ed Abbey invokes the material reality of the body to simultaneously challenge Thoreau and parody Shakespeare—no small achievement. Abbey knows not only that farts are funny but also *why.* Flatulence has been a perennial staple of literary comedy because of the remarkable power of a fart to explode human pretensions. And that is why we humorists keep our comic farts aimed directly at high culture— because a healthy ripper is an attack upon oppressive cultural authority and a powerful assertion of freedom and independence.

If the literary history of flatulence is distinguished, the natural history of farting is perfectly enthralling. Fart gas is composed of oxygen, carbon dioxide, and, for only about a third of us, nitrogen (whether nitrogen is present in our flatulence is a product of heredity, like the color of our eyes or hair)—as well as small amounts of the mercaptans and hydrogen sulfide that give butt burps their notorious stench. When we squeak one out, the vapor we release is produced by the air we gulp, gas diffused into our intestines from our bloodstream, and, most important, gas produced by the bacteria that inhabit our intestines and digest much of our food for us. In this sense every fanny bleat is the product of an amazing symbiotic, interspecies collaboration without which we simply could not survive. And here I paraphrase the poet Galway Kinnell's irrefutable scatological insight that those who don't poop don't live, while those who do do doo doo do. The same may be said of flatulence. As mammals, every one of us is living a Fart or Die existence.

You heard me right: *all* mammals fart. From packrats to mountain lions to whales. Turtles have exceptionally fetid farts. Termites are prodigious farters. Herpetologists can locate certain species of snakes by the unique odor of their farts. But among mammals farting is universal. Have you ever scanned the boggling diversity of the class Mammalia, that vast clade of endothermic amniotes, and wondered what unites us all? Well, I can tell you. It is the expulsion of intestinal gas through the anus. If you're a mammal, you're in the Guild of Flatus. You fart.

And if you're a human mammal, you fart a lot. On average, each of us produces a half liter of gas each day; scientific consensus puts the average daily numerical fart count at fourteen. And, ladies, don't blame the guys for peeling the paint. Although we men generally expel a greater volume of gas than you do, your flatulence has a higher concentration of the most odoriferous gases, so it all evens out in the end, so to speak.

The impressive frequency of human intestinal gas release—not to mention its telltale acoustic and olfactory potency—is obviously at odds with widespread social prohibitions against public farting. Never mind burning rubber in church or freeping during your own nuptials. Pretty much any gas expulsion—even popping a wee fluffy—is considered rude in almost all social situations. So much so, in fact, that public farting often leads to a secondary difficulty I refer to as "the problem of attribution." In a cowardly attempt to shift the blame we pin our poofs on the dog, or even on poor old grannie. We cough or scrape a chair leg to disguise the sound; we sidle away from the scene of the crime to flee responsibility for the stench. The problem of attribution has led to myriad—and for some reason always rhyming—fart blaming phrases. We all know "He/she who smelt it dealt it," but I prefer "he who deduced it produced it." If I'm in a casual mood I go with "the smeller's the feller." When I'm feeling intellectual I instead opt for "she who inculpated promulgated." There are also a variety of witty rejoinders to this kind of fart blaming. I'm especially fond of "whoever rhymed it crimed it."

When Hannah came of age for instruction in basic social etiquette, we taught her to say "excuse me" whenever she delivered a benchwarmer. But she didn't understand what we grown-ups know, which is that you say "excuse me" only once the cat is out of the bag. If you fart silently and expect to get away with it, then all etiquette bets are off. Not knowing this unwritten (and plainly hypocritical) social protocol, Hannah went around saying "excuse me" aloud all the time, which, because her flatulence was so quiet and inoffensive, was usually a mystery to other folks, who politely ignored her.

One day, however, my sister-in-law, Kate, asked in reply to one of Hannah's requests for pardon, "Excuse you? What for, honey?"

"I tooted, Auntie," Hannah replied, without a touch of shame or guilt.

Kate's husband, Adam, my brother-in-law, was so surprised by the frequency of Hannah's entreaties for forgiveness and so impressed with her unabashed candor that he suggested to Kate the brilliant idea that for a single week the two of them try the experiment of asking each other for forgiveness every time they did the one-cheek sneak. Adam specified that this obligation would remain in force whether they were together or apart. Always a gamer, Kate readily agreed, and an oath was sworn over wine. During the ensuing week there was a slew of gaseous emissions and admissions, the latter of which were duly confessed in person, by phone or email, or in text messages that read only "excuse me." It was a long week, and that is because Kate and Adam had to beg forgiveness for something on the order of two hundred farts. They simply learned by experience what every gastroenterologist knows: we vent a lot of steamers, and it is not only normal but in fact imperative that we do so. Farts, like love, are an inevitable by-product of our humanity.

Our social mores deem it perfectly acceptable for a person to publicly take out a paper-thin tissue and blow mucus out of their face holes. When we sneeze, which is far grosser because the mucus is being propelled at almost 100 miles per hour and can have a spray radius of up to five feet, people actually *bless* us. If I am *blessed* for publicly detonating a high-velocity snot shower, why must I beg pardon for farting, as if it were a crime? So ingrained in the culture is this shame and embarrassment that it has even given rise to so-called "flatulence underwear," the best-known brand of which is actually called Fartypants. The webpage advertising this forty-dollar product reads as follows: "Harnessing the same technology found in chemical warfare suits, these powerful pants are capable of stopping smells 200 times stronger than the average fart."

So here's the meditation with which I conclude this windy sermon. Why do we allow a little backdraft to send us reeling off into repression and humiliation, into the buying of underwear made to withstand mustard gas? Why are we obliged to be ashamed of this fine reminder of the astonishing interspecies collaboration that is the human body, this small but important thing we have in common not only with each other but with kings and popes, and with every fellow mammal from aardvark to zebra?

Thankfully, the emancipatory solitude of Ranting Hill allows me the liberty to fart *loudly*, though I still find it difficult to do what Benjamin Franklin would likely have preferred, which is to fart *proudly*. If Ben were alive today, he'd probably blast his butt bugle and then fist-bump everybody around. I know better than to take his advice on this one, so when I'm in town I begrudgingly conform to socially enforced fart suppression. But as a desert rat and a grateful denizen of these western wilds, I've learned to appreciate that the sound of a healthy ripper is still a small but unmistakable anthem to true freedom and independence.

THEM! AND US

Y OU MAY BE FORTUNATE, or, perhaps, unfortunate, enough
to recall the 1954 science fiction flick *Them!*, which, like the
radical environmental group Earth First!, had the audacity to include the exclamation point in its title. A classic fifties "Big Bug"
B movie, *Them!* concerns a colony of ants that is accidentally irra-
diated (as were plenty of Nevadans and Utahans during the same
period), producing mutated, monster-sized insects that rampage
through New Mexico, crushing skulls and filling friendly Westerners with deadly formic acid. The adventure ends in the subterranean labyrinth of L.A.'s storm sewers, where, after pinching off
a few human heads, the last of the creatures is destroyed, ensur-
ing Americans that they had nothing left to fear but nuclear Ar-
mageddon with the Soviet Union. As a cinematic romp through
Cold War anxieties, *Them!* gives us a monster to focus on other
than ourselves, whose monstrous intelligence produced the nuclear horrors that still terrorize us today. *Them!* somehow affirms
that it is easier to have your noggin compacted by the mandibles

of a giant ant than to come to terms directly with having let the atomic genie out of the bottle.

Here in the western Great Basin Desert we have our own *Them!*, known to entomologists as *Pogonomyrmex occidentalis*. At least for now, the western harvester ant is about a quarter of an inch long instead of fifty feet long. This is convenient, because this insect's venom has a lethal dose measurement of .12 mg/kg—a bug nerd's way of saying that it is comparable in toxicity to that of a king cobra. Much is made of the harvester's painful sting, but in my experience these guys do not attack unless you stand on them, which seems to me pretty reasonable. The sting itself is unpleasant, though I have never found it so severe as to be unresponsive to my famous "Three-Cold-Beer Remedy": apply one to wound, drink other two, repeat as necessary.

Most Westerners have seen harvesters before. They are common in this region, and their colonies exist within mounds that are unmistakably denuded of all vegetation in a circle with an eight- or ten-foot diameter. This removal of all growth prevents shading and facilitates thermoregulation within the colony's many tunnels, which extend down to the caliche—the desert hardpan that even the hydraulic auger on my tractor will not penetrate. We have lots of harvester colonies on Ranting Hill, but I have never found it necessary to exterminate them. The ants, which eat the seeds of desert grasses, are eaten by western fence lizards, which are eaten by Great Basin gopher snakes, which are eaten by red-tailed hawks—and if the economy goes south, I can always eat the hawks. Why antagonize cousin *Pogonomyrmex*? Even if there are fifteen thousand of them in each mound, they are still just wee little ants.

In early July, odd weather delivered an unusual, heavy rain on the heels of several days of very hot weather. On the day following the big rain, I noticed in our living room a few winged ants—an insect I had never seen around here before. Within moments there were many more ants than I could keep up with, even as I chased them around with the shop vac. Then, I noticed that something appeared to be moving behind the glass doors of the woodstove—a reflection off the glass, I thought at first. On approaching, however, I realized to my horror that the woodstove was seething with winged ants, which writhed against the glass by the thousands and wriggled out by the score. I sprinted out the front door and craned my neck to look at the roof, and that was when I had my *Them!* moment. Our tall chimney, which is stuccoed the color of desert sand, was now black with winged ants, whose countless millions and whose motivation for attacking our home remained equally inconceivable.

I sprinted back inside to see that hundreds of ants had escaped the stove in the time it had taken me to make my reconnaissance, and I realized, instantly, that I had a decision to make: I could continue fighting the ants a hundred at a time, until they filled our house, or I could take drastic action. In that instant I repositioned the shop vac, took a deep breath, and reached for the handle of the woodstove door, through which I now witnessed winged ants writhing in a foot-deep mass. Opening that door produced one of the ghastliest sights I have ever witnessed, as countless thousands of winged ants poured onto the hearth in a black wave, far exceeding my ability to control them, despite the vacuum inhaling at least fifty insects per second. Within five minutes ants were flying all over the house, but in that time I had also cleaned out the stove enough to ignite a few juniper sticks to make a smudge fire that stemmed further invasion from the chimney.

Because I'm the kind of natural history nerd who keeps the state entomologist's phone number handy, I soon had an answer to the question of why this vermin horde had chosen me as its hapless victim. As it turned out, the invading winged ants were our western harvesters, which had found the weather conditions perfect for swarming. The chief entomologist explained to me that when several days of scorching hot weather are followed by unusually heavy rains, both female and male ants from all surrounding colonies sprout wings and immediately engage in "hill-topping": they fly directly to the highest nearby point, which in this case was on top of the chimney, on top of our house, on top of Ranting Hill. There they formed "mating balls," an unfortunate term that accurately describes the orgiastic clusters of thousands of insects whose dangerous liaison had filled our home with insanely horny ants. The conclusion of this process is that any newly mated female who does not end up in the belly of a fence lizard, kingbird, or shop vac will fly to a new site, tear off her own wings, burrow into the ground, lay eggs, and perhaps found a new colony, of which she will be queen.

I have resisted the temptation to nuke the harvester mounds around our house, though in the wake of the ghastly invasion I confess that I was sorely tempted. But I do need to feed the lizards around here, and I also have a desire to see this bizarre ritual enacted again some hot, wet summer day. According to indigenous Pima mythology, our planet was created from a sphere of ants. Maybe I fear that to open the Diazinon is to uncork the genie's bottle right here at home, to rupture the silent bond that still abides between Them! and us.

SCOUT'S HONOR

ONE OF HENRY DAVID THOREAU'S many prose lines of pure poetry (his poetry, by contrast, is as prosaic as the side of a milk carton) sings that "the blue-bird carries the sky on his back." It is a line almost as lovely as the bird itself. The mountain bluebird, which is the state bird of Nevada, is a year-round resident here on Ranting Hill. The profusion of bluebirds here may be due to the unfair advantage the girls and I give them by mounting nesting boxes not only on our property but also (illegally, no doubt) on the public lands surrounding our home. There is hope in this small gesture of nailing little wooden homes into the tangled arms of junipers out here in the far reaches of the high desert.

Unfortunately, not all my associations with bluebirds are positive, for a bluebird restoration effort was my final merit badge project before being ejected from the Boy Scouts. To be more precise, I was formally excommunicated from scouting *before* managing to earn the "Arrow of Light," a rite-of-passage symbol that sounds like a cross between a cheap appropriation of Native

American mythology and a thinly veiled secularization of the ideology of a fundamentalist religious cult. I realize that in saying this kind of thing I am stepping over an invisible line in our culture. I mean, who rags on the Boy Scouts? Especially among those of us who deeply value outdoor experience and wilderness skills—not to mention less practical attributes such as trustworthiness and honesty—there is something sacrosanct about scouting.

Before failing to become a Boy Scout I was, under duress, a Cub Scout. I made it just far enough to become a "Webelo," which is scouting's equivalent of a "tween," a boy no longer a cub but not yet whatever is supposed to come next. A man? A bear? An eagle? A fake Indian? (Webelos are referred to as a "tribe," a designation my Northern Paiute friends fail to appreciate.) To make matters worse, *Webelos* was given the "backronym" of "WE'll BE LOyal Scouts," which served as yet another reminder that the fundamental principle of the organization was unremitting conformity and respect for authority.

I submit as further evidence of this hierarchical authoritarianism the "Cub Scout Promise," by which we were compelled to swear allegiance to God and country and to "obey the Law of the Pack," which sounded vicious and scary. Worse still was the "Scout's Law," which enjoined us to be "trustworthy, loyal, helpful, friendly, courteous, kind, obedient, cheerful, thrifty, brave, clean, and reverent." Is this a reasonable standard for any kid? I suspect most parents would be satisfied with, "Look, you don't have to be reverent or brave. Just stop hitting your brother."

As a boy I took seriously the moral imperative to achieve that long, aspirant list of noble traits, which is to say that I was from the beginning doomed to failure. Since scouting emphasized absolute respect for authority, it seems clear enough that profoundly anti-authoritarian nature lovers such as Emerson and Thoreau—never mind true radicals like Thomas Jefferson or Cactus Ed

Abbey—would have made abominable Boy Scouts, an observation that provides me genuine consolation.

Back in those days there was a lot of pressure on us little scouts. Lots of performance tests and social comparisons and merit badges earned or, more often, endless strings of minor failures that prevented the earning of badges. In retrospect, it all seems sufficiently ridiculous. Who even knows what it would mean to receive the merit badge in "Composite Materials"? Who really cares about achieving the "Coin Collecting" badge? (Better to earn the considerably more useful "Lifesaving" badge, so you can attempt to rescue your numismatist friends as they die of boredom.) How were we supposed to keep our priorities straight as we aspired to earn points within an organization in which "Dentistry" and "Nuclear Science" had equal value? How were we to decide between "Insect Study" and "Welding," between "Truck Transportation" and "Space Exploration"—all of which are actual merit badges?

It seems to me that "Wheelie Popping" or "Talking to Girls" or "Not Getting Your Ass Kicked by the Neighborhood Bully" or even "Fart Detection" would have been more useful than most of these merit badges. The value system of the entire enterprise appeared arbitrary and oppressive. If the camel was made by a committee, scouting seemed to have been created by a committee consisting of a Baptist missionary, an accountant, a government bureaucrat, a hippie back-to-the-lander, a marketing agency executive, a cigar store Indian, a New Age charlatan, and an undercover cop.

If you are speculating that the unhealthy energy around my not-so-warm-and-fuzzy memories of scouting suggests that I am protesting too much—that I am trying to cover up something—you are correct.

One lovely week during summer vacation, my all-white "tribe" of Webelos was on an extended camping trip, where we were commanded by Scoutmaster Williams, a man who took the "master" part of his moniker seriously. Master Williams was a "drop and give me twenty" kind of leader, though it was common knowledge among the boys that beneath his goofy uniform and hyperbolic Davy Crockett rhetoric was a plain old suburban dad, a henpecked, three-martini-lunch, lawn-mowing, golf-playing, midlevel sales guy. While the forest smelled of pure freedom, being there with Master Williams was a highly regimented and competitive experience. We boys wanted to explore the woods, to play hide-and-seek, scramble up rocks, and go fishing, but under Master Williams's leadership our experience was the opposite of play.

I do not exaggerate when I say that we could not dig a hole to take a dump without his turning the occasion into a competition—fastest hole, deepest hole, even *roundest* hole—and had there been a badge for meritorious defecation he would no doubt have adjudicated that contest as well. By the third night of the campout I had been forced to participate in so many competitions that I felt like an exhausted decathlete, only one whose events included boot waxing, dish washing, and melodic whistling. The only thing more frustrating than being forced to compete at whistling or scrubbing dishes was having my ass handed to me time and time again by the other boys, who seemed naturally to possess either the skills necessary to excel at such things or the sheer drive to humiliate me in head-to-head competition. It may sound silly now, but at age ten you do not want to be a loser every time, even if what you are losing at is whistling or digging a poop hole. Why couldn't I make that damned hole *rounder*?

On our third night, Master Williams arranged yet another competition, this one to determine who could build the biggest, best, fastest fire using only a single match. This challenge had everything Master Williams liked best: implied masculine potency, a pretention to survival skills, the drama of a winner-take-all race to the finish, and immense potential for the utter humiliation

HOW TO CUSS IN WESTERN

of the losers. The idea was that we would each gather our own materials—tree bark, twigs, pine needles, leaves—to lay and then ignite a fire that would, if we were truly skilled, be the first to leap high enough to burn through a sisal string that the master had tied tightly between two trees.

Master Williams blew his whistle to begin the first phase of the contest, a mere five minutes in which we fanned out into the woods to collect whatever we judged to be the most flammable and, therefore, choicest materials. Already exhausted, I headed into a thick stand of brush beyond the muddy spot where my own leaky pup tent was pitched and began to rifle through the duff on the forest floor in search of something dry enough to assure victory. But everything I gathered was thoroughly damp; even spruce cones and the cups of acorns felt moist clear through. A feeling of dread gathered in me, my chest tightening and my breathing accelerating as the seconds remaining to find something ignitable ticked away.

When Master Williams whistled the one-minute warning, I felt a wave of panic wash over me. It was in that moment of despair that I made the observation that would forever alter the trajectory of my career as a scout. I noticed, sitting near the mouth of my little green tent, the small red can of Coleman fuel we had used to refill one of the troop's cookstoves. Grabbing the can, I stepped behind my tent, squatted to the ground, and sprinkled some gas—and then a little more, just to be sure—onto the moist pinecones and twigs I had harvested from the forest floor. In that moment, I was not thinking of my pledge to be "trustworthy." I didn't *think* about what I was doing at all. Something in the reptilian part of my brain just *felt*—felt that I could not face another defeat after the embarrassing drubbing I had taken in the boot waxing and melodic whistling trials.

Arriving at the group just seconds in advance of disqualification, I now had five more whistled-off minutes to lay a fire, consisting of my pathetic little sticks and cones. I stooped to one knee and hunched unsteadily over the spot where I would be tested, trying with trembling hands to construct the ideal little teepee shape that was rising in front of the more capable boys working to my left and right. But the harder I tried, the more my little stick umbrella collapsed, and I could feel Master Williams's critical gaze fall upon me, even as a row of tidy twig wigwams materialized up and down the line. The tension was palpable and the concentration intense, because I knew what was at stake: to build a fire was the critical rite of passage into manhood.

At last the final whistle blew, and Master Williams counted down from ten, as if NASA were launching an Apollo rocket right there in the soggy woods. We ten truck-driving, tooth-filling, life-saving, steel-welding, coin-collecting, insect-studying, wood-whittling astronauts prepared for blastoff. Three . . . two . . . one . . . *ignition*! Up and down the line I heard the synchronized scratch and pop of ten individual wooden matches as they were simultaneously struck. Each boy knelt over his little stick teepee, lowering himself to touch the match to just the right spot of bark or twig. That single, tiny, flickering point of sulfurous fire was all that stood between triumph and humiliation, and I guarded mine as a kind of eternal flame, one that either would be extinguished in a moment or would burn brightly into manhood. I balanced awkwardly on one knee and bent forward slowly, lowering toward my malformed structure of twigs and cones, trying one last time, in my little, collapsing world of inferior whistling and inadequately dug holes, to keep my hopes from being extinguished. I chose a promising spot in my stick pile and lowered the match's small flame slowly toward it.

I do not remember the moment at which the match made contact with my little pile of damp sticks. I do recall that the resulting detonation sounded like a concussion grenade and that the rising fireball blew me backward onto my shoulder blades. There

HOW TO CUSS IN WESTERN

followed a welter of gasping and scurrying and, when I came to, a dim awareness that I was looking up through swirling smoke at the face of Scoutmaster Williams, who wore an expression of genuine concern. I was coughing a little, and the smell of singed hair was unmistakable.

"Son," he said at last, "you've burned your damned eyebrows off. Are you allright?"

I nodded yes, though I did not have the slightest idea.

"You're disqualified," he added, flatly.

I do not recall now whether I cried. The rest of my story is the unvarnished truth. Kicked-out scout's honor.

IMAGINING SHARK MOUNTAIN

THE OTHER DAY Caroline asked me, quite out of nowhere, a provocative question. "I know I'm five," she said, "but how old is the Earth?"

"Four and a half billion," I replied.

After being reassured that a *billion* is not, like a *zillion* or *cajillion*, a made-up word, Caroline had more questions. "How did anybody ever figure out such a big birthday number?"

"It all started with seashells on mountaintops," I told her.

"How did seashells get on top of mountains?" she asked.

"That's exactly what people tried to figure out for a few thousand years," I said.

Caroline persisted. "What did people think when they found the shells up there?"

"Well, some folks thought they were washed up by a big flood that's mentioned in the Bible, but a lot more people thought they just grew there, right out of the rock," I answered.

Now Hannah jumped in. "*Seriously?* How could anybody believe *that?*" she asked.

"Back then, nobody realized the planet was super old," I explained. "They just counted up the generations of all the people named in the Bible and reckoned that the Earth was about six thousand years old. And nothing in those six thousand years that they knew of could explain how seashells ended up on the tops of mountains."

"So how did they finally figure it out?" Hannah asked.

"With the head of a great white shark!" I answered enthusiastically.

Caroline, always obsessed with predation, was genuinely interested: "What! *How?*"

Now having the girls' full attention, I went ahead with the story. "During the mid-seventeenth century, some fishermen in Italy caught a huge great white shark. They chopped off its head and sent it by cart to this dude named Steno, who they knew was really interested in learning about nature stuff. When Steno studied the teeth of the shark, he noticed they were almost exactly like the teeth found on mountaintops along with seashells, and, in that moment, he made a giant leap of the imagination. Suddenly, he imagined a time in the deep past when those mountaintops were under the ocean, and had sharks and a lot of other cool things swimming around them. Steno realized that the only way seashells and sharks' teeth could end up on mountaintops is if the Earth is really, really old and has changed a whole bunch over time."

"Sharks swimming around mountaintops! They must have thought Steno was pretty cool for figuring that out," Hannah added.

"Actually," I said, "they thought he was nuts, and they were sure he was totally wrong. But, over the next couple of centuries, people figured out that he was right and that the Earth has had around four and a half billion birthdays."

Now, Caroline had a more practical question. "Are there any seashells on *these* mountains?" she asked, gazing out her bedroom window toward a serrated ridgeline of unnamed desert peaks.

"I'm not sure," I answered. "Should we check?"

"Yeah, let's go up there tomorrow," Caroline said, pointing. "And, in case we don't find any ocean stuff, let's take some of our own to leave up there."

The next morning, the girls sorted through a bag of seashells and sharks' teeth we had gathered several years earlier on a family trip to the Florida Everglades. They selected a few tiger and lemon shark teeth, some sand dollars, and several cat's claw shells, which they put into their daypacks along with sun hats, binocs, water, and enough licorice to allow us to survive the apocalypse. After eating a big breakfast of scrambled eggs, provided courtesy of what Caroline calls our "homemade chickens," we took Darcy the dog and headed up the brushy slopes west of Ranting Hill.

It was a typical summer afternoon in the foothills of the western Great Basin, which is to say that the Washoe Zephyr was blasting out of the canyons at thirty miles per hour, making it necessary for us to holler in order to be heard over the big wind. After hiking into a headwind for forty-five minutes, we paused on the dusty slope of the mountain to drink some of the well water we had slogged up the hill. Like any enterprising kid, Caroline had overpacked her daypack and then decided that I should haul it up the mountain along with my own. Just as I was offloading both packs to pause for water, an especially strong gust lifted a swirling cloud of sand and debris from the flank of the mountain and blasted it into my face. It felt as if a dump trailer of base gravel had been emptied into my left eye. No amount of blinking and dousing it with water seemed to help, and eventually I decided we would continue our mission even though I was now half blind. Caroline suggested, helpfully, that if my eye didn't heal I could wear a permanent eye patch, which she assured me would be "*totally* piratical."

Suddenly, I noticed that Darcy was nowhere to be seen. It was common for her to flush quail and jackrabbits, but this time she

HOW TO CUSS IN WESTERN

had not circled back, instead simply vanishing into the howling desert. We yelled for her, but the zephyr was so strong that our calls barely penetrated the roaring wall of wind, never mind crossing the expansive desert beyond. While the lost-dog-and-blind-dad misadventure was in full swing, the ocean of blooming rabbitbrush in which we stood had caused us all to begin sniffling and sneezing. We resumed our ascent, though by this point I had tied a bandana over my eye as a makeshift patch and was, as a result, off-balance and staggering. I was hoarse from screaming for Darcy, and I had no water to drink because I had poured the last of it over my face in a failed attempt to dislodge the gravel from my stinging eyeball. I was also wiping snot off my face with my sleeve—mucus I then accidentally transferred to my good eye, which became so red and itchy from wind, rabbitbrush, and snot as to no longer qualify as good.

At last we reached the summit ridge, where I flopped down in the lee of a granite palisade to gather myself while the girls did some climbing in the rocks. "Watch for rattlers, and don't put your fingers anyplace where a scorpion would hang out," I called, as the girls picked their way up through the granite boulders.

"We know, Dad," Caroline replied.

After a half hour the girls clambered back down, announcing they had discovered not a single seashell or shark's tooth. For my part, I was thirsty, tired, snotty, fretting about Darcy, and much in need of the Three-Cold-Beer Remedy for my injured eye. I declared it was time for us to leave our own seashells on the mountaintop. The girls unpacked their sand dollars, cat's claws, and sharks' teeth and located perfect notches in the granite, where they placed these ocean treasures as carefully as if they were religious icons being set ceremoniously into the niches of a temple wall. I snapped a few pictures to commemorate the event, and we turned our backs to the wind and headed for home.

Fortunately, Darcy was waiting for us back on Ranting Hill, though, unfortunately, she had passed the time by destroying my baseball glove, which she retrieved from the top of our picnic table. The ensuing moments continued the day-long comedy of errors. While yelling hoarsely at Darcy to drop my mitt, I tripped over a railroad tie and nearly impaled my formerly good eye on a bitterbrush branch. I then staggered inside, where in near blindness I immediately batted over the long-sought-for beer I had just opened. In frustration, I reeled away from the foaming mess and groped my way into the bathroom, where I removed my makeshift patch and emptied an entire bottle of optical saline into my injured eye. It later turned out to have been a bottle of nasal drops.

As I sat on the living room floor, sneezing and holding an unopened beer over my injured eye and an open beer in my free hand, I asked the girls, "How did you like our adventure?"

"I think it worked out great!" Caroline blurted. "We should name the peak where we left the ocean stuff. Let's call it 'Shark Mountain.'"

"Shark Mountain it is," I agreed.

"Sorry about your eyeball," Hannah added, "but that was pretty awesome putting those shells and teeth up there and thinking about Steno and the shark head and everything. I'll bet that, someday, thousands of years from now, somebody will find the stuff we left and wonder what happened."

"What do you think they'll guess?" I asked.

"It might take a long time of thinking about it," Caroline said, "but if Steno could imagine big sharks swimming around a mountaintop, maybe somebody will have a good imagination about it and figure out it was us. And even if they don't, they'll still have a mystery, and that's great too."

THE MOOPETS

I HAVE ALREADY bemoaned the four-letter word *cute*, but there is another four-letter word that, as a Nevada writer, I generally avoid using. It is a filthy word, one that immediately conjures up a range of unpleasant associations. To quote the character Eighties Robot in the movie *The Muppets*, "R–E–N–O. That spells Reno." I have the Muppets to blame for my need to use this foul word.

Not long ago, I was watching the 2011 film with the kids when, to my surprise, I glanced up to see a shot of the famous Reno Arch, an iconic landmark that spans the main drag of our downtown and reads, "The Biggest Little City in the World." That this odd equivocation is our city's official motto makes it clear that we've resolved to make a virtue of necessity by attempting to turn our community's identity crisis into a marketing coup. Is Reno a quaint town or a bustling city? Is it a family-friendly place or a den of iniquity? Is it an outdoor recreation hub or a gambling mecca? As our motto perhaps suggests, the answer to all of these questions is "Yes." But if we Renoites experience some confusion about our relationship to this place, it is at least a legitimate confusion that remains endlessly fascinating.

"Look, girls!" I exclaimed, pointing at our hometown on the TV screen. "The Muppets have come to Reno!" This was big news, because it suggested that our nearby city was about to get its fifteen minutes of fame—an outcome virtually assured by the fact that loving the Muppets is one of three things most Americans have in common (the other two: disliking paying taxes and thinking we sound good singing in the shower). Having your local town appear in a Muppet movie is like receiving the Good Housekeeping Seal of Approval, with the important difference that no one has read *Good Housekeeping* since 1959, while this Muppet flick has grossed close to one hundred million bucks.

I was also thrilled that Reno, which is a wonderful town but one with a nasty reputation, might at last be associated with something wholesome. In fact, the status of Nevada within the broader culture has not changed appreciably since 1862, when Mark Twain, who launched his literary career up on the Comstock in nearby Virginia City, characterized it as follows: "If the devil were set at liberty and told to confine himself to Nevada Territory, he would ... get homesick and go back to hell again."

Some might argue that we Nevadans have brought this dubious reputation on ourselves by pursuing the questionable economic strategy of legalizing whatever was or is illegal in most other places—by turns prizefighting, gambling, quickie marriage and divorce (not always in that order), prostitution, and recreational weed. But, for that one brief and shining moment, sitting with my beautiful daughters and watching Kermit roll into Reno in his Rolls-Royce Silver Spur, I imagined a possibility of redemption for our beleaguered little city. I even indulged the momentary fantasy that the Muppets, with their unimpeachable moral virtue, might help us to imagine a healthier, more virtuous relationship to our own home place.

But, as so often happens to people in Reno, my fortunes changed rapidly, unexpectedly, and for the worse. The film suddenly cut from the iconic Reno arch to an even more familiar site: a small, run-down casino on the north edge of town, a place I drive by each day while taking the girls to school. This particular casino's proximity to the local feed store, the rural liquor store, and a dilapidated taproom ensured my familiarity with it; this is my personal redneck strip mall. And although I have not had occasion to require the assistance of the bail bondsman whose storefront is just across the gravel parking lot, I find it comforting to know that he is close by in a pinch. Because the Muppets had fled the city proper for the broken-down, rural-urban edge, they were now on my home turf.

To appreciate why the Muppets' cinematic appearance at my local watering hole and poker parlor appeared so inauspicious, you need first to understand that Kermit's journey to northern Nevada is part of his heroic quest to get the old Muppet crew back together again to put on one last show, the proceeds of which will save the Muppet studios in Hollywood from the clutches of an avaricious oil baron. The charismatic frog's odyssey to reunite his troupe leads him to my local casino because the Muppets' stand-up comic, Fozzie Bear (the ursine humorist who, along with Henry David Thoreau, Mark Twain, and Edward Abbey, rounds out my personal quartet of patron saints), has fallen on hard times and has been driven to—of all the God-forsaken hell holes in the big West—Reno. Here, in the darkness on the edge of town, Fozzie has, in desperation, assembled the "Moopets," a second-rate Muppet tribute band consisting of unconvincing Muppet impersonators, including Miss Poogy, Kermoot, and Animool, the latter a cheap knockoff of the manic, hairy drummer

Muppet, who is here played with genuine panache by a real-life rock superstar, Dave Grohl of Nirvana and Foo Fighters fame.

The scene inside the casino reveals a vintage form of Reno despair so authentic and mundane as to be at once hilarious and disconcertingly familiar. When Kermit and his pals enter the derelict casino, Fozzie is already onstage with the flaccid Moopets, whose boredom is palpable. Surrounding the little stage are a few slumped-over, zoned-out patrons who are, if possible, even more jaded and apathetic than the half-assed tribute band itself. Several are certainly drunks; one may be a hooker. Singing a lame casino advertisement to the tune of the Muppets' celebrated anthem "Rainbow Connection," the stuffed bear croaks out a few uninspired lines:

Why are there such great deals
on our hotel rooms?
Free parking for cars, not RVs . . .

(*"Not RVs,"* chimes in Grohl, the grunge rock drummer turned fake Muppet backup singer.)

Our wedding chapel, is twenty-four hours,
No marriage certificate is needed . . .

At this moment, Caroline asked me if she could skip the film back and replay this song so she could master it in preparation for her elementary school's upcoming talent show. I winced and suggested that we save that project for another day.

The painful Reno stereotypes pile up thick as alkali dust once Kermit and Fozzie retreat to the bear's "dressing room," which turns out to be nothing more than a paltry scattering of crappy furniture in the open alley behind the little casino. As the frog and bear speak awkwardly of what Fozzie's life has come to, we hear in the background five pistol shots, followed by a police siren, squealing tires, and a cop on a bullhorn yelling, "Step out of the vehicle!" Given this alarmingly impoverished landscape, Kermit, stammering as self-consciously as an amphibious Woody Allen, expresses concern for his friend's destitution. For his part, the bear puts on a brave face, responding, "Look at me: I'm living the dream!" This ironic outburst is followed immediately by a flash of lightning, a peal of thunder, and a sudden downpour—clearly metaphorical weather, since you would sooner draw to an inside straight than see a thunderstorm around here.

Grasping at a last scrap of pride despite his abysmal condition, Fozzie tries futilely to console both himself and his web-fingered pal: "It's allright, Kermit, it's not your fault. We had a good run." And with this grim assessment, the now not-so-comic bear incisively encapsulates the Reno experience. The message is unmistakable: my town is the final whistle-stop on a one-way trip to Nowheresville. Reno is depicted as the place where dreams—even sweet and innocent Muppet dreams—come to die.

My girls quickly recognize the familiar exterior of the casino, though of course they have never been inside. "Hey, isn't that right across the street from where we got the baby chicks this spring?" asks Caroline.

Big sister Hannah has a harder question: "Dad, is it really like that in there? All smoky and dark with not very good music and people asleep at their tables?"

"No . . . not really," I replied. "Well, kind of."

"Hmm," said Hannah, processing. "That doesn't look very fun."

Caroline followed up, excitedly, "So the Muppets are right about Reno after all!"

"Well . . . not really," I said, a little defensively. "OK, sort of. Well, OK, yes. Allright. I guess the Muppets *are* right about Reno."

In that moment, I realized that one reason we Renoites have such a troubled relationship to our place is because we feel compelled to resist stereotypes that are sometimes accurate. It was also a difficult moment because I could see the girls trying to renegotiate their own relationship to place—struggling to reconcile a landscape they love with the satirical version of it rendered by Kermit and his crew. For the girls, our home desert exists within a wild, magical world where beauty expresses itself daily, effortlessly. What could it mean that their hometown was now Muppet shorthand for the place you land in life only when all decent options have been exhausted?

This challenging parenting moment forced me to revisit the vexing question of how I should respond to the negative stereotypes that plague our little city. One approach is to fight back with facts: Reno has a vibrant arts community, a beautiful river corridor, incredible weather, and amazing access to desert and mountain wilderness. It is a city full of nice people—independent, unpretentious people with solid common sense who do not try to convert you to anything. My hometown is a place where you can order a rye Manhattan without having to explain that you don't want a damned maraschino cherry in it. Or, I could take a different tack by pointing out that folks who live here can take a joke and, for that reason, appreciate the brilliance of the Muppets' parody of us. After all, we really *are* the biggest little city of the pathetic tribute band. Performances here have included Who's Bad (Michael Jackson, though the name says it all), Live Wire (AC/DC, the "blunder from down under" resurrected), One Night of Queen (not a transvestite cabaret show, though we have those too), Voyage (a faux Journey, which was a band so atrocious that even a knockoff must be an improvement), and Eliminator (not the brand name of a laxative but instead the fake ZZ Top, complete with the mega-beards they made cool a generation before *Duck Dynasty*). We Renoites really do know how to laugh at ourselves, which explains why so many of us went into mourning when Comedy Central's classic mockumentary TV series *Reno 911!* folded way back in 2009.

But, after ruminating on my conversation with Hannah and Caroline, I've decided that I'd rather defend Reno within the terms of the negative stereotype that plagues it. I think again of the real place that is parodied in the Muppet movie. Some of the folks inside that old neighborhood casino may be past their prime, but they are still welcomed. There is a unique kind of tolerance there, where the down-but-not-quite-out find a temporary home. You can't tell a millionaire from a bum in that place, which suits me fine, since I look like a bum and would just as soon have people wonder. Maybe folks from hipper places think we can't separate the wheat from the chaff around here—that we aren't smart enough to judge winners and losers. Then again, maybe we are and just don't. Reno may have earned its bad reputation, but it has always been the land of the second chance, the place where the down-and-out Fozzies of the world come for one last shot at redemption. "Could be, might be, maybe this time, maybe next time," wrote Jill Stern, who described Reno as "a symbol of the second chance and the chance after that which every man always believed awaited him."

Remember this important point: Reno keeps Fozzie off the street until he is rediscovered. And that is the part of the Muppets' send-up of our town that I treasure the most. It is here that Fozzie lands when he has no place to go, when he is utterly without prospects. This is precisely what allows Kermit to rediscover the ursine comic, whom he recruits to reenter a life of fame and fortune. Fozzie is no doubt back on Broadway now, but without Reno, who knows? Nobody wants to contemplate a Muppet suicide or overdose. Besides, I've been sleepy over a beer once or twice in that little casino myself, listening to a musician or comedian who had not had their break yet, or who had it long ago and was trying for that mythic, long-odds comeback. Any town might have given Fozzie his first big break, but only Reno could give him something more precious by far: a second chance. Who in hell would want to call Reno home? Well, as Kermit croons in the Muppets' signature tune, "The lovers, the dreamers, and me."

DESERT FLOOD

EVEN IN THESE extremely arid lands, where desiccation is a condition to which we're well accustomed, the severe drought of the past few years has been especially troubling. Recently, though, we've had the opposite problem: not too little water but far too much of it, and in too little time. A series of unusual summer thunderstorms has hammered our desert hills, fueling flash floods. You might think that a lot of rain is a good thing in a place that receives so little of it, and perhaps an ennobling metaphor like "quenching the land's thirst" might rise to mind. Once you've witnessed a flood in the desert, however, a very different metaphor suggests itself. Imagine being so parched that dehydration is a real threat to your survival, and then being offered a sip of water from a forestry hose blasting at 450 psi; you'll get your water, but it will likely take your face off with it. Needless to say, this choice may cause you to ask yourself: "Am I really *that* thirsty?" As my fellow desert writer Craig Childs put it in his book *The Secret Knowledge of Water*, "There are two easy ways to die in the desert: thirst or drowning." According to the US Geological Survey (USGS), in American deserts more people drown than die of dehydration, which puts the immense power of flash floods in humbling perspective.

In weather-nerd parlance, a "flash flood" is distinguished by speed as well as volume: it is an event in which geomorphic low-lying areas are inundated in less than six hours. This event can be triggered by torrential rains or accelerated snowmelt, or by the collapse of an ice dam—or an artificial dam, as when 2,200 people were swept to their deaths in the 1889 Johnstown Flood in western Pennsylvania. While we don't tend to associate deserts with water, flash flooding is not only surprisingly common but also especially dangerous in desert areas. The unstable temperature and pressure gradients that characterize weather patterns in arid lands can create a lot of water in a short time. Desert soils, both sand and clay, are poorly suited to slowing and absorbing water, and in an open, mostly treeless landscape like ours there is little vegetation to stanch the flow. While heavy rain falling on a forest is much like water pouring onto a sponge, a torrent in the open desert is more like a deluge splattering onto a rock.

Because this landscape does not have regular rains to help keep ditches, culverts, and drains clear, floods here tend to be heavily laden with debris, which creates blockages that exacerbate water damage. This effect is clearly visible on our rural road here in Silver Hills, where the recent flash floods uprooted sagebrush, Russian thistle, and tumble mustard, jamming them into the mouths of culverts, where they formed a mesh lattice that captured mud, clogging the culvert heads, impeding water flow, and causing the runoff to jump the ditch and rip across the road surface, where it sliced through the roadbed, rendering it impassable. Most surprising and hazardous, flash floods in the desert often occur beneath clear skies. Localized thunderstorms somewhere in the upcountry release the water load, which gathers force as it tumbles downslope through canyons, arroyos, and washes, eventually blasting into areas where no rain may have fallen—where, in fact, the sky may be clear and the sun may be shining brightly.

I had a memorable experience of this kind of flood thirty years ago while backpacking in the Escalante Canyons of southern Utah. If you've never seen this magnificent country, it is perhaps best imagined as an immense labyrinth of fissures carved into the exposed face of a vast expanse of mesas and plateaus. For the hiker, navigating these canyons means meandering through a maze of narrow slots, beneath sheer walls of Navajo sandstone painted with carbonate patina and streaked with the impressionistic tracery of desert varnish. The narrowness and depth of these sinuous canyons create their undulating beauty but also ensure that those of us walking within them have little idea what might be going on beyond the slice of sky we're able to see between the looming rims of the canyon's sheer walls.

On the day I witnessed the surprise flood, bright sun illuminated the red cliffs of the canyon I was tracing, while the sliver of sky visible above me remained pure azure, save for an occasional, puffy alabaster cloud drifting innocently across it. Despite these ideal conditions, by midafternoon I heard the distant rumbling of thunder, which was my cue to peel a weather eye and devise contingency plans. After hiking for another hour I reached a bottleneck in the canyon, and I knew that in entering it I would risk being trapped without an escape route in the unlikely event water was running somewhere above me and beyond my sight. Instead I decided to wait it out, remaining in a wide amphitheater of the canyon bottom, through which the small creek slid first against one wall, then snaked gracefully across the cobble of the broad wash to run gently against the other wall. I sat down on a sandy bench that seemed safely elevated above the creek, leaned back against my pack, and enjoyed the beauty of the place.

After a half hour I noticed the little creek begin to rise, and rather quickly. Within minutes, water that had been only inches deep—so shallow that I had simply walked through it perhaps twenty times that day—rose to a foot deep, while also quickening its pace. Then, roaring around the bend of the canyon, came the aptly-named "snout," the leading wave that is pushed before a flash flood. It was several feet high, viscous and brown, loaded with debris, and barreling into the canyon with a volume and force that far exceeded anything the little creek could contain.

I grabbed my pack and clambered up to a broad notch higher in the cliffside. From there I watched as the coffee-colored snout led a wave that swept the canyon bottom, overrunning the shallow creek bed and spreading out over rocks and sand, tearing through reeds and bushes, encircling boulders and swirling around the trunk of a large cottonwood tree that had formerly stood thirty feet from the creek. I watched in amazement as the canyon of dry cobble became a cliff-to-cliff river, shallow but roiling, spitting chocolate foam and plowing forward with a tumbling load of upcanyon debris.

In the next moment, something equally remarkable and surprising occurred. The sky darkened as I heard the wind rise and felt the temperature plummet. And then the rain that had been heralded by the flood exploded above me in a cloudburst so intense that it hammered the cliffs in deafening sheets. Water also began to run down the canyon walls and spout from their tops. Within moments the canyon bottom was being pounded by a series of spontaneous waterfalls, as the mesa lands above funneled the runoff and shot it over the canyon's sandstone brow. Squinting through the blast I counted eleven simultaneous waterfalls, one of which was launching from the cliff beneath which I had sheltered, catapulting itself over me and into the canyon-wide torrent below.

In less than ten minutes the dramatic downpour ceased, and one by one the waterfalls shut off. The expansive sheet of spontaneous river below me retreated toward the creek's banks, leaving water standing in pools and debris heaped against the shoulders of boulders and the boles of cottonwood trees and up high in the tangled arms of willow thickets. It was difficult for me to process what had just occurred, not only because I had never seen anything like it but also because the force and power of the flood were matched by its incredible speed. An immense volume of water had arrived suddenly, blasted the canyon, and vanished, all in what seemed a matter of moments.

The massive thunderstorms that hit northwestern Nevada this summer packed a similar punch. Worse still, these storms rolled through in a tight series, reducing the land's capacity to absorb additional water, and tearing into areas where mud, silt, and debris deposited by other recent storms had already created obstacles to drainage. Our flash floods were smaller than those that ripped through the Front Range of the Rockies in 2013, and they were minor compared with epic events like the 1976 Big Thompson Canyon flood in Colorado, when a foot of rain fell in a four-hour period, creating a twenty-foot-tall snout that scoured the canyon, killing 143 people who were unable to reach higher ground in time. Among those drowned was Sgt. Hugh Purdy, whose heroism is sung in "Here Comes the Water," a beautiful, heart-wrenching ballad by the Zen Cowboy, Colorado musician Chuck Pyle.

But if the recent flash floods here in the western Great Basin were less deadly than these historic floods, they were nevertheless dramatic by local standards. Some area locations received more rain in two or three days than they normally see in a full year, and a few saw the better part of their annual allowance in a matter of hours. Up on Ranting Hill we were slammed by five major rainstorms within the span of a week; no old timer I've talked with here in Silver Hills can recall anything like it. The gravel road we use to reach our home was blown out in many places, its ditches full, its culverts buried, and its gravel surface swept out into the sagebrush flats. The roads on the nearby public lands fared much worse. Most became flowing torrents, and are now sliced through by erosion gullies three feet deep. In other places on the Bureau of Land Management (BLM), arroyos that I have hiked through hundreds of times, and which have never even appeared moist, ran at least four feet deep with surging water.

When we think of floods, we tend to picture rivers swelling, cresting their banks, and flowing out across floodplains. But here in the environs of Ranting Hill our situation is markedly different, for we have no rivers, streams, creeks, or rivulets—nary a trickle. There are a few hidden seeps and springs, and one endorheic lake bed, but no surface water. In an environment such as this, the spontaneous appearance of creeks and rivers is as remarkable as was the sudden birth of eleven waterfalls on that strange, beautiful day down in the red heart of the Escalante. A flood here is a matter not of a river rising but rather of a river appearing where none has existed in recent memory, and then vanishing almost as abruptly.

The marvel of a desert flash flood is intimately related to our incapacity to register environmental change that occurs on temporal scales that are uncalibrated to human perception. Although I've taken more than two thousand hikes on the public lands adjacent to Ranting Hill, I have never observed water in any of the arroyos, those dry, arterial gullies that run through the parched desert like a mysterious system of ancient, long-abandoned aqueducts. For that reason, I have come to imagine a desert shaped by deep time, by slow, incremental change that I will never possess the longevity or acumen to observe—the kind of change produced by wind sculpting rock. In their sudden appearance and disappearance, and in the profound changes they have wrought in my home landscape, these flash floods have reminded me that this astonishing place has been shaped by sudden as well as gradual change. To see this land for what it is I must learn to view it as a vital, pulsing labyrinth of desert ghost rivers—rivers that will flow with wind and light only for another twenty or fifty or a hundred years, when they will once again rage with the rare bloom of a sudden, unseen cloudburst.

WHAT WOULD
EDWARD ABBEY DO?

O NE CRISP, BLUE DAY last fall, I dodged work to climb my home mountain with three friends who were also shirking their adult responsibilities that day. My buddy Steve was with us, a guy who has not only a huge heart and a thousand skills but, more important, a farting donkey named Flapjack. "Flappy," who also goes by "Flatchy" (as in "flatulence"), has the unique ability to fart loudly, be spooked by it, which in turn causes him to fart, and . . . well, if you sit on Steve's corral fence on a sunny day with a six-pack, you will discover the true meaning of the term "quality entertainment." Also with us was a French visitor to the Great Basin, a guy whom I'll call "François" not only because that is the ideal name for a Frenchman but because, by happy accident, that is his real name. My friend Rick was also passing through, sneaking in a trip to the high desert before hunkering down for another long winter in his wet corner of the Northern Rockies.

The four of us had enjoyed a perfect day atop the mountain, 8,000 feet up in the cerulean Nevada sky. We had seen pronghorn on the run and some nice late-blooming wildflowers and had even found a chipped, obsidian arrowhead when we stopped for lunch in a high meadow ringed by aspen and mountain mahogany. On our way back down the mountain that afternoon, we paused to drink at a small seep on a very steep face. While resting there, Steve noticed a hip-high boulder that he observed was perched precariously on the slope. "I'll bet a couple of guys could roll that thing," he said. Everyone was quiet for a moment.

"Maybe," I replied, "but even if a couple of guys *could* roll it, they *wouldn't* roll it. Would they?"

"Good question," Rick said. "If a couple of guys—let's say four guys—*could* roll that boulder, *would* they?" I suggested that it might be helpful if we each imagined reasons why a few hypothetical guys should not roll a boulder down a mountain.

"Could hit somebody?" Steve asked. I explained that this was impossible; I had just scanned the canyon below through my binocs, and it was entirely free of humanoids, just as it had been every time I had hiked this mountain in the past decade.

Rick then suggested, with a straight face, that moving the boulder could represent interference with the perfection of the natural order and might disrupt some divine plan as yet beyond human ken.

"But what if moving the boulder is *part* of the divine plan?" Steve responded. Everyone nodded in agreement.

"And you guys know what they say about gravity?" I added. "'It's not just a good idea; it's the law.' Would the divine natural order be guided by the law of gravity if huge rocks weren't *supposed* to tumble down mountains?"

"Besides," Rick added, "the uplift in the Sierra is raising this mountain two or three inches a year, so whatever a couple guys might do would be fixed pretty soon anyhow." Once again, everyone nodded their assent.

"On the other hand," I said, "that old coyote Sisyphus was tortured by the gods for messing with their order, so a few guys might meditate on his terrible punishment before doing anything rash. Then again," I added, "Sisyphus was in trouble because he got it on with his own niece. You guys don't plan to get it on with your nieces, do you?" Three heads shook emphatically from side to side.

"And speaking as a guest here," Rick continued, "I should remind y'all that Sisyphus also killed his guests. You don't plan to kill me, do you?"

"Not unless I run out of gorp," I answered, glancing involuntarily in the direction of Donner Summit.

Steve now noted that "a couple of guys don't know for sure if they *could* move that thing. Look at the size of it." We all gazed again at the big rock.

"True, but it's incredibly round," Rick observed. Yes, we all agreed, the boulder Sisyphus had left on the pitch of my home mountain appeared uncannily round. It seemed *made* to roll.

"OK," I said, "but my main concern is that, if a few guys rolled a boulder off this mountain, one of them might say something like, 'Let's rock and roll' or 'That's just how we roll.'"

"We absolutely can't have that," Rick said sternly.

"No way," Steve agreed. François didn't say a word, but the expression on his face made clear that he was perfectly disgusted by the idea that anyone would contemplate saying such a thing.

We all sat in silence for a very long time, and we were all staring at that boulder, and I suspect we were all thinking the same thing: grown men—responsible men, men with jobs and mortgages and families, dedicated environmentalists—do not roll boulders down mountains. Yet there we were, all staring intently at that immense rock.

"Well, gentlemen," I said at last, "we've reached an impasse. I suggest we consult an international expert. François, with the notable exception of wine and cheese, your people have done nothing for our people since the battle of Yorktown. What do you have to offer us now?"

"Whenever I am uncertain," replied François, in a thick French accent so utterly authentic that it sounded hilariously fake, "I ask myself but one question: W W E A D?" When he had finished pronouncing each letter with meticulous emphasis, the three of us looked at him quizzically. "What would Edward Abbey do?" he explained coolly.

It was a beautiful moment, one in which absolute clarity had come to all of us at once. Without saying a word, the four of us stood up, walked over to the boulder, dug the toes of our boots into the mountainside, and began to push with all our might. The giant stone budged slightly, rocked a bit in its socket, and then, incredibly, started to roll very slowly. It soon picked up speed, however, and as the rock sped down the mountain, it began to leapfrog, launching itself off ledges, ramming and blasting apart other rocks, striking sandy slopes and snowfields on its unstoppable, half-mile-long, 1,600-vertical-foot plunge to the valley below. The boulder was racing now, each impact causing it to leap a great distance before landing again, and with every touchdown a cannonball explosion of rock, sand, and snow blasted high into the air. Each impact elicited a collective gasp or cheer, and I can't begin to explain how cathartic it was to watch that big rock fly. I felt as if I had been rolling a boulder up a mountain my whole adult life and had now simply stepped aside and just let it go.

It took a long time before the boulder came to rest in the valley, its magnificent, explosive, kinetic energy expended. We then tracked its route down the mountainside, following the footprints of a stony giant that had raged through snow and sand and sage. To our amazement, we found that some of the impact craters were several feet deep, and they were sometimes as far as forty feet apart. The boulder had not *rolled* down the mountain at all but had bounced and flown down it. After an hour of picking our way along the boulder's path, we at last came to the rock itself, resting serenely and alone in a sagebrush flat out beyond the mouth of the canyon. Here, we all sat together around the rock, staring at it as if it might still go somewhere.

I hike that canyon often, and I can report with authority that the boulder has not yet moved. It has, however, cast a shade so rare that it is already nurturing sprigs of bitterbrush and chokecherry—plants that will do their small part to transform this granite bene-factor into desert soil. "Let the gentle bush dig its root deep and spread upward to split one boulder," wrote the people's poet, Carl Sandburg. The temporal scale on which we operate makes it hard for us to see that this rock, once rolling, is still on the move. Time will tell where it might go next. Roots or ice may fracture it. An earthquake may tumble or swallow it. The glaciers may return to carry it off. Or, it may simply melt away into the invisible, slow-motion, time-lapse photography of wind.

LONE TREE

I T IS OFTEN SAID that we cannot see the forest for the trees, but that is not a problem out here in the western Great Basin. In moist slot canyons or riparian areas you will find aspen, cottonwood, mountain mahogany, ponderosa and even Jeffrey pine, but the open country is sagebrush steppe, largely treeless high desert where the "forest" consists only of widely dispersed Utah junipers. It is hard for most of us to conceive of a forest in which individual trees may be hundreds or even thousands of yards from each other, due to a lack of water. Our trees are like distant electrons within the vast, burning nucleus of the desert; this is a forest consisting mainly of space.

"Language makes a mighty loose net with which to go fishing for simple facts, when facts are infinite," wrote Edward Abbey in his introduction to *Desert Solitaire*. "If a man knew enough he could write a whole book about the juniper tree. Not juniper trees in general but that one particular juniper tree. . . ." In the high, open valley west of our home, which is all public land, there is one such particular juniper tree. It is not a very big tree, a young juniper, perhaps only a century old. Most remarkable about this tree is its isolation, as it stands alone on the floor of this expansive valley. From any hill or mountain ridge in the basin you can look down and see, in some cases from vast distances, this single juniper, standing solitary, a tiny island of green in a sea of shimmering sage. Abbey's wisdom notwithstanding, I have no desire to write a book about an individual tree. But this one particular juniper—which I call Lone Tree—surviving in isolation out on those baked, windy flats, has earned itself legacy status.

The proper way to stalk a tree is to begin from a great distance, uphill and downwind, and then sneak up on it very slowly. I begin my approach to Lone Tree by climbing the three ridges my family has named Moonrise, Palisades, and Prospect, each higher than the last, that rise westward into the azure sky above Ranting Hill. From the crest of Prospect I gaze west over a jumble of boulders and out across the sweeping valley to our imposing home mountain, which rises above it. At this distance, Lone Tree is visible only to the eyes of one who already knows where it stands. Because the tree is more than a mile away and 1,000 feet below, it is a mere pixel, indistinguishable from other dots on the landscape, most of which are jumbles of granite boulders.

After descending the western slope of Prospect through a steep canyon, a half hour of scrambling brings Lone Tree close enough that, while still impressively distant, it is now discernible as a tree rather than a heap of shattered rock. I am still a half mile from the juniper and 500 or so feet above it, and I can tell it has not yet noticed me. This is an important distance from which to admire Lone Tree, because if you happened to be perishing of exposure, that tiny mushroom out on the sage flats would represent your only possibility of refuge from the desert sun. It is impossible to

HOW TO CUSS IN WESTERN

imagine seeing this green magnet from here in summer and not fantasizing about repose in its cooling shade.

Another twenty minutes of billy-goating down a slope that is by turns scree and sand brings me to the valley floor. I am now a quarter mile or so from Lone Tree, and I am better able to sneak through the sage, prowling low like a mountain lion. From this proximity, a distinct color palette emerges. The sidereal blue of the western sky is brushed with the diaphanous white of attenuated clouds, while the mountain below it is sere brown and corrugated, here and there shadowed by rock fields on north-facing slopes. Because I now have an eye-line view of the tree, I notice how beautifully it is set against the double-knolled hill behind it. That mounded rise is topped with boulders that, apparently, host enough chartreuse lichen to provide a hint of a yellow-green that is mirrored in a few ephedra bushes in the foreground, scattered among the dust-colored sage. From this angle and distance, Lone Tree is irresistible. I zigzag stealthily through the sage maze toward its welcoming shade.

Once I am within a hundred yards of the tree, what appeared to be lichen on the rocky hills behind it emerges, instead, as small bunch grasses growing in open patches in the hill's broken granite tops. At this distance, the shapes of the image strike me as even more important than its colors. This perspective reveals how gracefully the domed arch of the juniper's crown is repeated in the arched tops of the granite hills behind it, which are themselves reflected in the sinuous bulges in the ridgeline of the big mountain that fills the western sky. From here I see, for the first time, that the tree has a full crown but a skeletal, open structure beneath. I am struck by how this form is mirrored in the brushy tops and dark stems of the big sage that fills the valley. This top-heavy shape shows that Lone Tree has been cropped around its base, perhaps by grazing mule deer when it was just a sapling.

From thirty feet away, Lone Tree fills my view, crowding out the landscape and demanding my full attention. Darcy, the dog, has run ahead and is already reclined comfortably beside it. At this distance, I detect hopeful second growth spouting from the long-ago cropped trunk. The area beneath and surrounding the tree is clear of sage, suggesting that this juniper beacon provides shelter for open range livestock, for Old Man Coyote and other wild things, even for a wayward desert rat and his old dog.

Noticing a dark mass hidden within the tree's crown, I make my final advance on this particular juniper. Now standing beneath Lone Tree and looking up inside it, I see cradled in its angular, scaled arms a large, intricately woven stick nest about eight feet off the ground. I do not know who lives in this nest, but I do know why: if you fancy an arboreal home, this is the only game in town. The nest leads me to the realization that this tree has accomplished something remarkable. It is growing in an exposed and unfavorable spot and has, at some point, been thoroughly munched. It has allowed many of its limbs to die in a successful attempt to preserve its core vitality. Miraculously, it has even escaped the wildfires that scour this valley every fifteen or twenty years. Working entirely alone, this single, gnarled juniper has kept my scorching, windswept home valley from being treeless. I should be fortunate to achieve so much in my own life.

I spent a pleasant half hour with Darcy, both of us stretched out in the sage-scented alkali dust beneath Lone Tree. Only when we finally rose and shook ourselves off did I suddenly notice the other tree. I had made a pilgrimage to this solitary tree only to discover that it was not alone after all. Just to the north of this particular juniper was its shadow tree, a filigree of shade cast down for the benefit of every creature in the valley. It is this single juniper's cooling shadow that makes it possible to traverse the valley floor during midday in summer. We stop at Lone Tree because it is all that can be put between ourselves and the sun. Beneath it you will find owl pellets and mustang dung, the coffee-bean droppings of pronghorn, coyote scat containing polished fragments of kangaroo rat skulls, tufts of matted jackrabbit fur, the gracefully curved alabaster rib bone of a calf, a pair of ragged raven feathers, an old beer can pull tab carried in from afar by an enterprising packrat.

Our way of seeing the world is conditioned not only by experience and belief but also by scale: by the distance, angle, and perspective from which we approach and view things. I find it useful to back up from something I am concentrating on—a problem, a memory, an essay—until I am so far away from and so high above it that it exists in that liminal zone between the visceral world of granite and the equally beautiful universe of the imagination. I also find it helpful to begin from far away and high above something I hope to explore—an idea, a way of understanding the desert, a lone juniper—and stalk it through registers of scale, until it becomes solitary, focused, all-consuming. Perhaps the true nature of a desert is veiled by its sage-filled valley, and the nature of its valley is hidden within the arms of its solitary juniper tree, and the nature of that unique tree is concealed within its woven nest, and the nature of that singular nest is a latticed pattern so exquisitely imbricated and minute that one must begin from a distant ridgetop in order to see it clearly.

HOW TO CUSS IN WESTERN

RECENTLY I WAS shooting the breeze with a friend when, as is my habit, I casually described a prominent politician as being *chickenshit*, while also characterizing this representative's disingenuous, self-serving prattle as *horseshit*. To my surprise, my buddy looked at me quizzically and requested a clarification of the distinction between the feces of a chicken and those of a horse. This struck me as a low point in the history of human communication. After all, it ought to be immediately apparent that *horseshit* is *bullshit*, while *chickenshit*, a different matter entirely, is moral cowardice. What had become of our ability to curse effectively, let alone colorfully? If we cannot communicate through the use of profanity, I wondered, what the hell is left? Have we been reduced to sonnets and tweets?

That evening, over a stout tumbler of High West Rendezvous Rye, I decried the profound illiteracy of my well-intentioned friend, whose lexicon of scatological euphemisms was so tragically impoverished. Instead of supporting me, as a good life-partner should, my wife, Eryn, turned the tables by suggesting that I curse too much. "Are you shitting me?" I asked in shocked reply. "I'm a writer, honey. I invoke profanity only when driven to it by an absolute need for expressive precision."

At this point, owl-eared Hannah and Caroline joined the conversation from down the hall, affirming loudly that "Yeah, Dad cusses *way* too much!"

My further protestations precipitated the girls' suggestion that we set up a "swear jar," the proceeds of which we agreed to donate to Animal Ark, our local wildlife rehabilitation center.

"Fine," I replied. "Name your price. And prepare to break the bad news to that crippled sow bear that she'll have to suck her paws this winter, because they won't be able to buy her a dam . . . a *damp* apple with what I'll be putting into that jar. Poor thing. She just loves damp apples."

It was soon decided that each swear word would require a fifty-cent contribution from whomever should so utterly lack self-control as to let it slip. I learned a lot in that first week of living with the swear jar. First, I discovered that I have absolutely no verbal self-control and that my reliance on profanity is not only excessive but perfectly astonishing. It soon became clear that the contents of the swear jar were on pace to eclipse the girls' college savings, and that was without a single contribution from anyone else in the family but me. Worse, I learned that it was impossible for me to pay only four bits per curse, because immediately upon swearing I would recognize my error, which would cause me to swear anew. So it was a one-buck minimum every time I slipped, which occurred approximately twice each waking hour. And, by the way, I'm an insomniac.

I like to think of myself as a New West kind of guy, but all this regulation and penalizing of what I view as an essential mode of self-expression caused me to wonder what the tradition of profanity in the Old West might have been. Well, I looked into it, and it turns out that the pedigree of swearing in the West—and such swearing was once referred to with the beautiful phrase *airin' the lungs*—is in fact quite distinguished. Profanity, slang, vernacular, and hyperbole were once woven deeply into the fabric of western life and manners. In fact, many of the flamboyant expressions pioneered by early cowboys, miners, gamblers, prostitutes, and others are still part of our American lexicon. We all know what it means to be a *bad egg* or to be *bamboozled* or to have a *bee in your bonnet*. And even if we forget the difference between *chickenshit* and *horseshit*, we remember what it means to be *buffaloed*, to be in *cahoots*, or to get something done by *hook or by crook*. After all, if you don't *cool your heels*, you might end up *dead as a doornail*. You may have *a hard row to hoe* (note to Millennials: *row*, not *road*), but if you *have a mind* to *pony up* instead of being a *skinflint* and *making tracks*, you might end up with enough *coin* to *shake a stick at* instead of winding up *tuckered out* and *mad as a hornet*.

Gold miners taught us that although we all want to *hit pay dirt*, not everything we attempt in life will *pan out*. Cowboys reminded us to first *hold our horses* and then to *strike while the iron is hot*. Trail cooks suggested, none too politely, that we should *quit our bellyaching*. Sheepherders helped us see what it means to be *on the fence* or *dyed in the wool*; they also crafted their stories into *yarns*, which they *spun*, sometimes in order to *fleece* the listener. As a writer and a certified curmudgeon, I especially appreciate that early printers expressed the feeling of being *out of sorts*—a term that refers to the grouchy mood brought on when a printer runs out of letters while setting type.

It might be just as well that we have let a few of these old sayings fade into trail dust. For example, it may be wise that we no longer refer to facing a difficult undertaking as *having big nuts to crack*. All in all, though, we have lost more than we have gained. I wish we still referred to procrastination as *beating the devil around the stump*. I'd like to be able to say, when I am in a hurry, that I am about to *mizzle, burn the breeze, spudgel, light a shuck, marble, cut dirt, put my licks in*, or, best of all, *absquatulate*. And why should I apologize for having forgotten something when I might instead say that I *disremembered* it—a term that is more honest, since my selective memory is actually a subversive form of passive resistance? For example, I seem to routinely *disremember* Caroline's elementary school talent shows—where, if I were so unfortunate as to remember them, I would be subjected to an interminable lineup of kids breathlessly shrieking out awful pop songs in voices that could *worm a sheep*.

As I began to *lamp* that, if I did not *mend my ways* and *hobble my latchpan*, I was going to be *in for it*, I *fetched up on* the idea of just *blathering* western *'til the cows come home*. (Translation: observing that, if I did not change for the better and be quiet, I would get into trouble, I decided to speak in western slang constantly.) That way I could say exactly what I had on my mind, do it forcefully and colorfully, and not have to arrange for direct deposit of my paycheck to the damned swear jar.

My second idea was to cuss out my boss, just to *catch the weasel asleep* and *acknowledge the corn* (surprise him by speaking the truth about his shortcomings). I will *swear an oath* that this *big bug* is *crooked as a Virginia fence* (testify that this self-important oaf is corrupt); truth told, the scoundrel could *swallow a bag of nails and cough up corkscrews*. He is *so weak north of his ears* that he *couldn't hit the ground with his hat in three throws*, so ugly he'd *make a freight train take a wagon trail*, and *so mean he'd steal a fly from a blind spider*. So I swaggered into his office and *set to frumping him for a shanny* (began mocking him as a fool).

"Tom," says I, "you're a *no count flannel mouth chiseling chuckleheaded gadabout coffee boiler* (no good, smooth-talking, dishonest, ignorant, jawflapping, lazy ass), and if you *reckon* you can *fob* me out of my *oof* with your *rumbumptious monkey shines*, then you've *got the wrong pig by the tail*. (If you think you can con me out of my money with your arrrogant tricks, you've picked the wrong man to mess with.) I'm *reverent* as a *kedge gully washer* and *death on slimsey, rag-propered lickfingers* like you. (I'm powerful as a big storm and dangerous to feeble, overdressed ass kissers like you. And here I pause to interject that *lickfinger* is undoubtedly the greatest euphemism for obsequiousness ever invented.) I will go at you *hammer and tongs* and *exfluncticate* you all to *flinders*, until you *plain hang up your fiddle*. (Reader, you have this one, right?) Well, Old Tom was not only *difficulted* by my *sayings* but downright *funkified*, so I just *sidled* out of his office with a satisfied *squinny*. (He was both perplexed and scared—yes, *funkified* means scared!—by what I said, so I walked coolly away with a contented chuckle.)

I was feeling *above snakes* from *getting the drop on* my boss with my *pink* westernized lingo, so I *trampoosed two whoops and a holler* over to the *watering hole* to *check* my *capital bar dog*. (Happy at having insulted my boss with my brilliant regional vernacular, I strolled to the nearby bar to visit my favorite bartender.) "Dondo," says I, bustin' through the swinging doors of the Risky Biscuit Hayseed Saloon, "you know *plain right* that I'm a *dabster lapper* (know very well that I am an expert drinker), and that I'm here to get *corned* (tipsy), *fuddled* (slightly drunk), *slewed* (moderately drunk), *whittled* (quite drunk), and, directly, *full as a tick* (very drunk). *Bend my elbow*, partner! *Set me up* (pour me) some of that *anti-fogmatic* (whiskey), *tanglefoot* (whiskey), and *snake poison* (whiskey), and bust out some *bumblebee* (whiskey), *clinch mountain* (whiskey), and *coffin varnish* (whiskey) to boot! I am *going whole hog* (all the way) to *paint my tonsils* (drink), until I'm *roostered* (extremely drunk) and *snapped* (thoroughly drunk), so spread out a *general treat* (a free round) of *pop skull* (whiskey), *jack of di-*

amonds (whiskey), *prairie dew* (whiskey), and *rebel soldier* (whiskey) for these here *lushingtons* (fellow drinkers). Set up the *red eye* (whiskey), *bottled courage* (whiskey), *rookus juice* (whiskey), and *oh-be-joyful* (whiskey) for every last *poke down the rail* (person at the bar). Now, Dondo, *go at it like you're killing rattlers* (energetically)! *Crate up* the *sheepherder's delight* and *tarantula juice* (put away the cheap whiskey) and bust out some *dynamite* (whiskey) and *neck oil* (whiskey). You know I won't *shoot the crow* (leave the saloon without paying), so put up the *washy stingo* (weak beer) and get the *scamper juice* (whiskey) and *family disturbance* (whiskey) flowing! *Liquor me on sheep dip* (pour me whiskey), until I've got a *brick in my hat* (am unthinkably drunk) and I wake with *roaring case of barrel fever* (a massive hangover)!

Well, I carried on in that style of *blusteration* for twenty minutes, until I had used up all sixty-seven of the westernisms for whiskey that I had recently learned. When I was finally through, Dondo just handed me a cup of black coffee—and his *hoothouse blackwater*, by the way, *could float a pony*—and then he phoned Eryn to ask her to come pick me up.

The downside of my experiment with talking western was that not even my family—or, more important, my bartender—could understand a word I was saying. The upside was that I was able to *air my lungs* without being fired, or even having to pay into the swear jar. In fact, I soon took up a more disciplined approach to western cussing, adopting such stock terms as *crimany*, *jiminy*, *pshal*, and *I vum*. But my favorite curse, one that is authentic to the Old West and to which my own identity drew me magnetically, is *I Dad!* I don't know what it means, but I know from experience that it is true. Sure, I cuss too much. Sure, I'm ornery as a cross-eyed mule. But even with all my flaws, *I Dad!* Even my daughters agree.

I *reckon* at this point I've *gone to seed. Certain* I have been out in the high desert so long *I know the lizards by their first names.* And maybe Eryn is right that it would be better if I just plain dropped the wonderful expression *hot as a whorehouse on nickel night*. But right there it is anyway, because I don't *cotton* to *buckling under* when it comes to *hammering out ace high* literary art. Until the day I *cash in* and *get planted* in the *bone orchard*, I am going to *keep after* being a *scrapping slang whanger* who *goes across lots* to *string a whizzer* for y'all. And if I do *swack up* a *stretcher now and agin'*, I'll *ride a long slipe* to *be a buster* who's *a huckleberry above a persimmon*. And that, pardner, ain't no *horseshit*.

DESERT RIVER MUSIC

Reno is a desert town with a river heart. The Sierra Nevada snow-fed Truckee River, which is the only outlet from nearby alpine Lake Tahoe, passes through our little city on its 121-mile-long slide out to Pyramid Lake, which is among the most spectacular desert terminal lakes on the planet. Although the Truckee is the lifeline between these two gorgeous lakes, which are separated by 2,500 vertical feet, it has not generally received good treatment as it passes through the center of this western Great Basin city. Once an old cow town attempting to shift to a new resort economy, Reno had turned its back on its river corridor, choosing instead to focus visitors' attention on the impoverishing entertainments offered just around the corner, where casinos sprouted up along Virginia Street. The river, so nearby, was relegated to a concrete trough with few access points. Its riparian zone became home to hobo camps, while the Truckee itself was regarded as little more than a thing to be crossed on one of the city's old bridges. For a long time our river gave sacred water but received profane treatment.

This denigrating view of the Truckee has mostly changed these days, with a series of ambitious and largely successful river core urban renewal projects. We now have a whitewater park, pedestrian bridges, improved access, and more greenspace along the floodplain. And while all this exists in the shadow of towering casinos, it offers a helpful reminder that we desert rats should pay tribute to the Truckee, without which our survival in this arid place would be tenuous. Even in the desert, a city without a home river seems to me a lonely proposition. I'm grateful that we've begun to appreciate ours.

Twenty years ago, before the Truckee corridor through Reno had been revitalized, I used to hang out down by the river a lot. At that time I wasn't married, didn't have kids, and had not yet begun to build our home up on Ranting Hill, far north of the city and out in the remote, high-elevation canyons and ridges along the California line. Back then I was a new arrival in the Great Basin. My desert rat whiskers had only just begun to sprout, and I still felt more comfortable keeping water in view.

It is with the bittersweet sensation of a lost place and time that I revisit in memory those old days and nights along the Truckee. One of my closest friends at that time was Brad, a guy whose aplomb and cool had earned him the nickname "Smoo B" (as in "Smooth Brad"). I had plenty in common with Smoo B, but perhaps most important was our love of playing music together, something we did at every opportunity. He picked guitar and I blew blues harp, and we bonded over the fact that neither of us had ever met a note we didn't want to bend. As a little, two-man jam band we played out at cheap bars now and then—the kinds of dives that were adjacent to tattoo parlors, and once we even played an acrid-smelling saloon that slung both rye and, in the back room, skin ink. One-stop shopping for Harley dudes. We never used the same band name twice, and I've forgotten all of them now save "Jeebies and Stankeye." I no longer recall how we

HOW TO CUSS IN WESTERN

came up with that name, or which one of us was which, or if we even stopped to ask such questions at the time.

One unexceptional summer day, Smoo B and I agreed to meet down by the river in the late afternoon, just to pick and bend a few notes before dark. We sidled along the Truckee for a while before sitting down on an old concrete landing near the south buttress of the Virginia Street Bridge, in the heart of downtown Reno. A double-arch gem built back in 1905, this bridge became famous in legend as the place from which newly liberated women tossed their wedding rings after finalizing a divorce in the nearby court-house. In *The Misfits* (1961), John Huston's immortal cinematic tribute to the loss of the Old West, a fragile Marilyn Monroe considers doing just that.

Smoo B led, and I followed, as he unfolded a spontaneous set of river music: a surprisingly relaxed take on Neil Young's "Down by the River," followed by a meander through Bob Dylan's "Watch-ing the River Flow," which segued magically into B's crazy, mel-low cover of the Talking Heads' cover of the Reverend Al Green's classic "Take Me to the River"—a tune he strummed with a stac-cato rhythm that made it sound like it was being laid down by Bob Marley rather than David Byrne.

"Dip me in the river / Drop me in the water / Washing me down / Washing me down." As Smoo B finished those lines and looked up, and I lowered my harp from my mouth and opened my eyes, we both noticed something curious. While we were jam-ming, three people had planted themselves on the landing not far from us. There was an older man, a middle-aged woman, and a very young man. They looked as if they knew one another, and yet they did not quite seem to be together. They appeared to have been attracted by the music, but despite a few furtive glances our way, they made no eye contact with us as they sat staring toward the afternoon light rippling on the river. All were shabbily dressed.

The young man had a grimy backpack and bedroll, the woman a bulging, oversized canvas sack, the older man a plastic garbage bag half full of crumpled aluminum cans. It was clear enough that they were homeless. Here, in the long shadow of the casinos, lived the river people whose luck had run dry.

I slapped the harp on my thigh and wiped the face of its wooden comb across my jeans to give myself a moment to think. Then I looked at Smoo B and tipped my head in the direction of our audience. B smiled and nodded.

"We're worried y'all can't hear us very well from over there," Smoo B called to the strangers. "We've got some more river music coming up. Want to join us?" The three looked over with surprise and then, with only a slight hesitation, stood up and made their way over to us. With no further words Smoo B built on the earlier reggae vibe with a sweet, lilting strum through Jimmy Cliff's "Many Rivers to Cross," which he nodded for me to sing. I couldn't remember the first verse, so I began with the second: "Many rivers to cross / And it's only my will that keeps me alive / I've been licked, washed up for years / And I merely survive because of my pride." By the time we finished the song, three or four other homeless folks had joined the audience; word was spreading among the poor people residing in the willow thickets and beneath the bridge overpasses of the Truckee River corridor.

Smoo B launched into a short, reckless version of Johnny Cash's "Five Feet High and Rising," though neither of us remembered many of the words. B recalled "The chickens are sleepin' in the willow trees / The cow's in water up past her knees," and I dug up "The rails done washed out north of town / We gotta head for higher ground," but mostly we just threaded out a lonesome jam, the end of which was met by an audience that had once again doubled in size. Although we had fumbled the tune badly we still received generous applause, and there were smiles everywhere when B, while retuning, said with a grin, "Could be that one needs a little work. Well, any requests?"

After a pause, a homeless man who appeared to be in his early forties spoke up. "How about Springsteen's 'The River'?"

"Can you help us out with those lyrics?" I asked.

"Sure can try," the guy smiled back. B launched into the tune, and the man sang the sad ballad with genuine feeling, never missing a word. I choked up a little as I tried to nail the harp solo coming out of the final verse, which, given both the singer and the situation, was heartbreaking and poignant: "Now those memories come back to haunt me, they haunt me like a curse / Is a dream a lie if it don't come true, or is it something worse?"

When we three finished the tune, congratulations were offered all around, and the crowd of more than a dozen people now seemed to have grown more comfortable with an experience that was as unusual for them as it was for us. An older woman, who referred to us kindly as "boys," offered us a heel of bread that she had wrapped in a tattered, green bandana; a man, grasping a brown paper bag, explained that he had traded a little day labor for vodka and that we were welcome to pull from it if we liked. Thanking them for their generosity we asked again if there were any requests. A white-bearded older man, who appeared to be in his late seventies, laughed a loud, raspy laugh that revealed how few teeth he had remaining. "Let's have some hobo songs!"

The request was so gracefully ironic and well-timed, and was delivered with such enthusiasm and good humor, that everyone laughed together in a bonding moment that slung a bridge across a broad river of class, opportunity, and life experience.

"Well, sir, we can handle that one," I replied, returning the man's smile with my own.

"How about a Woody Guthrie set?" Smoo B offered. There was general agreement on the plan, and we began the most memorable string of songs I've ever had the pleasure to play. I no longer recall all the tunes that set contained, but we hit "Hard Travelin'" and "Goin' Down the Road Feelin' Bad," "Vigilante Man" and "Do Re Mi," "I Ain't Got No Home in This World Anymore" and "Pretty Boy Floyd the Outlaw," which includes the following immortal lines:

> As through this world I've wandered,
> I've seen lots of funny men;
> Some will rob you with a six-gun,
> And some with a fountain pen.

The folks in the audience thanked us after each song, asked if we were sure we didn't mind playing just one more, offered us bites and swigs of what meager food and drink they possessed. They tapped their feet, clapped their hands, sang along when they knew the words, and greeted the last note of each tune with grateful applause.

We played on toward dusk. Smoo B's fingertips were turning to hamburger from playing so hard for so long, and my lower lip had begun to bleed from ripping notes on the harp. Now dark began to fall in earnest, and B proposed that he and I each choose one song to conclude the spontaneous musical event that our audience had already begun to refer to as a "concert."

For his finale, Smoo B chose the playfully upbeat "Big Rock Candy Mountain," the ultimate celebration of a hobo's imagined paradise:

> In the Big Rock Candy Mountains
> All the cops have wooden legs
> And the bulldogs all have rubber teeth
> And the hens lay soft-boiled eggs
> The farmers' trees are full of fruit

And the barns are full of hay
Oh I'm bound to go
Where there ain't no snow
Where the rain don't fall
The winds don't blow
In the Big Rock Candy Mountains.

We all finished the song laughing together, no doubt wishing as we laughed that the pastoral fantasyland of the Big Rock Candy Mountains might yet be a real possibility for us.

Now the time had come for me to choose the closing tune. In that moment of falling darkness I named the melancholy "Hobo's Lullaby," and through the taste of blood laid down the sweetest, most languid harp notes I think I've ever produced. I had no way of knowing at the time that this would, many years later, be the tune with which I would sing my baby daughters to sleep.

Now don't you worry about tomorrow
Let tomorrow come and go
Tonight you're in a nice warm boxcar
Safe from all that wind and snow.
So go to sleep you weary hobo
Let the towns drift slowly by
Can't you feel the steel rails hummin'
That's the hobo's lullaby.

When the trailing notes of this last lullaby had lilted and riffled down the Truckee, and we had all returned from the world that only music can build to the stark reality of the homeless encampments along the darkening riverside, our audience not only applauded but now gave us a standing ovation. There were more offerings of the food and drink that were so precious to them. One lady said it was the best afternoon she had experienced in years. A younger woman invited us to come back any time, adding with a sweet smile that "We don't get too many concerts down here." And then, in what was the most touching moment of this strange and wonderful experience, a man in tattered, greasy clothes offered us what I suspect was the greatest gift he had to give. He asked, with a note of genuine concern in his voice, if we had a safe place to sleep, adding that he knew a secret spot where we could be sheltered from both weather and harm. "I don't tell anybody about it," he whispered, "but after what you did for us here it seems right to offer."

SHIT HAPPENS

I MIGHT AS WELL come right out and admit it: I lost my septic tank. The tank is twelve feet long, five feet wide, and five feet high. But that didn't stop me from losing it.

I suspect you've never heard of John Mouras, but you owe him a greater debt of gratitude than you might imagine. In the 1860s, Mouras, a Frenchman, designed the first functional septic tank, thus introducing a simple, highly effective technology that would, by century's end, come into wide use and profoundly improve the lives of people around the globe. Before Mouras's tank, human waste was often dumped out of windows from chamber pots and drained away through open gutters. But even when waste was gathered into hand-dug cesspits, it still contaminated groundwater, spread disease, and smelled horrible. The writer H. L. Mencken reportedly claimed that Baltimore in the 1880s reeked "like a billion polecats." Even in the twenty-first century, people have been killed by drowning or asphyxiation in collapsed cesspits. One moment you're mowing the lawn; the next, you've been sucked into a sixteen-foot-deep subterranean chamber dug by some long-gone person who needed a place to put their poop. I'm keen to avoid an inglorious end in which I leave this fine world in an archaic fecal storage chamber.

Fortunately, John Mouras's invention changed all that, and it is to his credit that the septic tanks we use today don't differ appreciably from his prototype. Waste is delivered through pipes into the two-chambered tank. In the first chamber, solids settle and are anaerobically digested by bacteria, a process that radically reduces their volume. Liquid then flows into the second chamber, where further settling occurs. The resulting, second-stage liquid, now relatively clear, is safely returned to the soil through a network of perforated pipes laid out below ground in a large area called a leach field. That's the simple, elegant system in a nutshell. It isn't rocket science, but it works. And it certainly beats the smell of a billion polecats, not to mention offering the handy side benefit of making it unlikely that you'll contract hepatitis, typhoid, or cholera.

If, like most Americans, you live in a city, it may be unclear to you why I'm singing the praises of an underground human-waste–digesting tank. Please understand that for those of us dwelling out here in the sticks, the septic tank remains the only feasible alternative to the chamber pot or cesspit. In fact, about a quarter of American households still depend on the lowly septic tank, whose glory has unfortunately remained unsung. Lest you urbanites begin to feel superior, remember that—to crib from the title of a children's book Hannah and Caroline loved when they were little—*Everyone Poops*. Your poop, like mine, is removed from a toilet through a pipe that takes it away. But where is "away"? Although you don't tend to think about it when you flush, an impressively complex network of pipes delivers your feces to a distant wastewater treatment facility. In fact, there is an entire profession devoted to dealing with your poop. You're thinking "Wastewater Treatment Engineering," aren't you? That does sound comfortingly antiseptic and professional. Try again. *Fecal Sludge Management.*

I've evangelized about the miracle of the septic tank and reminded you that your magically vanishing poop doesn't go "away" but is instead shunted through an elaborate arterial system of conduits that eventually deposits it where it becomes the focus of some other guy's day job. (Your sewer bill doesn't seem so unreasonable at this moment, does it?) But my real point is that when you live as remotely as we do, there simply is no "away" to which things may be thrown or flushed. We are alone and largely self-contained up here on Ranting Hill. Everything we need must be brought in, while everything we want to dispose of must be hauled out. This self-sufficiency extends to our own feces. Rather than going "away," our waste simply makes a short journey from our bathroom to a nearby underground tank, where it must occasionally be dealt with by our family's designated Fecal Sludge Manager.

Unfortunately, I am not a very adept Fecal Sludge Manager, and that is how I came to lose the damned septic tank. You see, the tank must be pumped out about every four years (for some reason I tend to think of it around the time of presidential elections), because septic sludge overflowing the tank into the leach field is environmentally harmful, and it is my responsibility to prevent that mishap. Step one, then, is to dig up the tank and expose its twin lids (which resemble manhole covers) in preparation for pump out. Because I keep meticulous files on every aspect of our modest little Ranting Hill kingdom, I began by fetching the folder labelled "Septic Tank," which I felt certain would identify the precise location of the underground poop reservoir. When I opened the file folder I instead discovered only the following three notes, scrawled in my handwriting by the idiot who had dug up the tank four years ago:

"Tank hard to locate. Major ass pain."

"Great Basin Tectonic Event IPA is DA BOMB. Get another growler!"

"Write about this someday. Angle: odor of shit. Shit and memory. *Remembrance of Things Past*. Like Proust with his madeleine. Only shit."

These barely intelligible ravings gave me absolutely no sense of where to dig. However, I thought I had a decent memory of the tank's location, and so I began to excavate with shovel and mattock. It was necessary to dig by hand rather than using our tractor, because the septic tank is plastic, and one accidental strike with the teeth of the backhoe's bucket would crack it, leading to a very messy, stinky, and expensive replacement project. While the tank is immense and should be a breeze to find, the problem here was one of depth as well as location. Because we dwell atop a steep hill, anytime we need a flat spot we must create it by hauling in fill dirt and leveling it to construct a terrace for whatever we hope won't blow, roll, or slide off into the sagebrush below. In this case, we had decided three years ago that the girls needed a trampoline. To create a flat spot for this ridiculously large toy, I had hauled in a lot of fill, which meant that in addition to not knowing where the tank was, I had also lost track of how deep it might now be buried.

Well, I dug a hole. And then another, and a third, a fourth, and, eventually, a fifth. Then, on the theory that I simply wasn't digging down far enough, I enlarged and deepened the holes, one after another. At this point I had gone three feet deep, when a septic tank would normally rest only a foot or so beneath grade. Five monster holes, each with an immense pile of shoveled dirt heaped next to it, and no sign yet of the tank. My back was about to give out, I was frustrated that my notes had been useless, and I also had some choice words for the trampoline. (And, yes, I did say these things out loud to the trampoline, as if it could be dressed down by my blue-streaking profanity.) At dusk I threw in the towel, put up my tools, and headed for a cold beer—a beer that, much like the excremental sludge in my missing septic tank, had been created by a process of fermentation.

"How did it go out there?" Eryn asked, as I reached into the fridge.

"Well, if I keel over with a coronary from all this digging," I answered, "you'll have five pre-dug holes ready to go. Bury me in whichever you like."

"Five holes? I thought you were just digging up the septic tank," she said, innocently. There followed a long, awkward pause.

"I can't find it," I confessed.

"Isn't it pretty big, like the size of a car?"

"Yes, dear, it is," I answered.

"Well, Bubba," Eryn finally said with a shrug, "shit happens."

In her brilliantly titled book *The Grass Is Always Greener over the Septic Tank*, the humorist Erma Bombeck advised that we should all "Laugh now, cry later." Under normal circumstances this is precisely the kind of wisdom I endorse. But another great humorist, Will Rogers, observed that "Everything is funny, as long as it's happening to somebody else." And it was Uncle Will's insight that seemed to apply here, as I just couldn't manage to laugh at my own absurd predicament. For the next few days, every time I used the toilet I imagined what was flushed racing through unseen pipes to "away," some yet undiscovered location where it would plunge into a 1,500-gallon slop bath of urine and feces. How could a guy lose something like that?

The next day I used the tractor to drag the trampoline about twenty-five feet away, and I then began to hand-dig beneath where it had stood. I dug four big holes that day and three more the day after that. By the fourth day, there was more hole than ground in the vicinity I was working, and so many perfectly symmetrical piles of excavated dirt that it looked as if the place had been infested by a scurry of man-sized ground squirrels. Or, perhaps, as if a band of pirates had come and gone seeking buried treasure—albeit pirates whose treasure map consisted of nothing more than a nearly illegible note remarking enthusiastically on the excellent flavor of Tectonic IPA.

As I stood surveying the damage I had wrought, and wondering what I should do next, Caroline came outside to bounce on the trampoline. "Whoa, Dad, look at all those holes. That's *epic*! What are you making?" she asked.

"Nothing, honey. I'm trying to find a buried treasure called the septic tank," I said.

"Which hole is it in?"

"That's what I'm trying to figure out," I replied. "Which hole do *you* think it's in?"

"Hmm. Which one did you dig first?" she asked. I surveyed the dozen holes and pointed to the one I had excavated at the start of my misadventure. "OK, that's the one," Caroline said with absolute confidence. "You know how you always say I gotta trust myself? Something in your dad brain told you to dig there. Maybe you just gave up too easy. I bet it's right under your nose!"

Caroline's advice, though unscientific, wasn't any less rational than the haphazard strategy I had pursued on my own, and it was considerably more thoughtful than any of the notes in my own folder on the subject. So, as she stood watching, I clambered down and resumed digging in hole number one in search of a tank full of number two. Within five minutes, my shovel struck with a hollow thud I had not heard in four years. I tossed the tool out of the hole, bent over quickly, and began desperately scratching at the soil with my gloved hands, like a coyote pawing the desert sand for water. *Eureka*! I beheld a telltale swatch of emerald-green, high-density polyethylene plastic that was the tip of the fecal iceberg I had worked so hard to find. After thanking Caroline for her help, I dug on with the fervor of a jackrabbit, and in less than two hours I had fully exposed both lids of the tank in preparation for the pump out.

The next afternoon, a large truck rolled up to Ranting Hill to make my family's excrement go "away." Technically called a "fecal sludge vacuum tanker," this specialized truck is, for a reason that is as obvious as it is ironic, casually referred to as "The Honeywagon." With a capacity of nearly 15,000 gallons, it can transport the contents of a dozen septic tanks at once, and it is usually driven by a burly young guy named Jimmy, who, despite what he does for a living, is inexplicably cheerful. On this day, however, I was surprised when a short, gray-haired, older woman threw open the door and climbed down from the cab of the truck.

"Mike, right?" she said, shooting her small hand forward for a shake. "Jimmy's laid up with his back again, so I'm makin' his runs today. I'm Sue, his mom. Let's get this party started!" With that she gazed out over my field of holes, in the center of which sat the exposed lids of the tank.

"Tell you what, Sue," I offered, "I'll pop those covers for you if you don't tell Jimmy about my treasure hunt. You just say I hope his back mends soon."

"Deal!" she said, with the same cheerfulness I was accustomed to in her son. She stood nearby and watched me crawl into the hole and begin to unscrew the tank lids that, for a just a moment longer, would continue to separate the pure desert air from the accumulated vapors of a presidential election cycle's worth of gases produced by decomposing human waste.

When the first lid came off, I felt as if the proverbial billion polecats had sprayed me all at once. It didn't even feel like a *smell* but rather like I had been struck in the face with a solid object, like a board or brick. My eyes began to involuntarily twitch and water, my lips curled back from my teeth like those of a neighing horse, and a coppery tang filled my mouth as my throat seized and my knees turned to rubber. I must have wobbled a little, because Sue called out, "Hey, Mike, you OK? You can't smell the methane, but that ammonia gets your attention, doesn't it? And the hydrogen sulfide can knock you right on your patootie!"

When I replied, unconvincingly, that I was fine, Sue handed me a long metal rod with a flattened piece of steel welded to its end. "Time for the fun part, Mike. You get to stir!" she said, enthusiastically. I stood frozen, gazing up at her in disbelief. "Come on, Sugar, dip that paddle in the soup! Easy-peasy. Just like a milk shake. Gotta stir first so you don't leave delicious chunks of fruit on the bottom when you start sucking through that straw. You want to get it all!" I continued to stare at her blankly. "You like milk shakes, Mike?"

In that milk shake moment, I made up my mind that I no longer gave a shit what Jimmy might think of my misadventure. I felt an instinctive urge to bail on this stinkfest before gray matter began to ooze out of my earholes. Never mind polite terms like *pungent*. I was now withering in the full olfactory blast of a skeevy, blechish, frowsty, purulent, fetid, barfled, mephitic, pustular, feculent, nastified funk stew beyond human imagining. It took only that moment for me to learn what was worse than losing the septic tank: finding it.

Then, just as I was about to climb out of that hole for good, Sue made one final observation. "Well, Mike," she said in a tone of genuine sympathy, "I know this isn't a ton of fun, but look at it this way: you made it." She was smiling the whole time, and there was not a hint of sarcasm in her voice.

Even in that moment of my greatest trial, the simple words *you made it* left me without a legitimate counterargument. We teach Hannah and Caroline to clean up after themselves, to be

HOW TO CUSS IN WESTERN

self-sufficient, to take responsibility for their own messes, both literal and figurative. What then was my option in this moment? Make an old lady climb into a putrid hole and stir a tank full of feces not of her own making? I might have handled this situation as do her other customers, by rationalizing that she gets paid to do this work—that she deserves the shitty end of the deal because she agreed to trade some of her time for some of my money.

To my way of thinking, the virtue of dwelling in this remote desert place is that it so often brings us into unmediated contact with visceral realities that are obscured by other modes of living. In choosing to make a life here on Ranting Hill I also chose to remove, to the degree possible, what stands between myself and nature—between myself and reality, my own body, and the physical demands of this hard, beautiful place. And even if I didn't fully understand what I was signing up for at the time, I don't intend to ask for my money back now.

"Ain't that the truth, Sue," I choked out, as I began to stir. "Ain't that the truth."

SIR RANTSALOT IN THE DEAD TREE FOREST

WHY AM I, a confirmed desert rat, about to offer a paean to cutting trees—to cutting them first down and then up? The answer may be found in the intimate relationship between this desiccated, largely treeless arid landscape and the nearby Sierra Nevada Mountains, whose eastern slope is carpeted with conifer forests comprised of a variety of lovely tree species, among them white, red, and Douglas fir, incense cedar and western juniper, and ponderosa, Jeffrey, lodgepole, and sugar pine. One of the many advantages of our proximity to the Sierra is that it makes it possible for us to augment the warmth produced by our highly efficient passive-solar home with heat generated by burning beetle-killed, sun-dried trees.

I have always loved to fell, limb, buck, split, haul, and stack wood, and I have been heating with wood most of my adult life. There is something deeply satisfying about making a pilgrimage into the forest and returning with a fruit so precious that it flowers a year later in the gentle, blossoming flames that warm my daughters as they play or read by the hearth. Think of it as the thermal equivalent of preparing and eating vegetables grown in your own garden. That may be a sentimental take on a backbreaking form of labor that is performed amid the roar of a chainsaw and the smell of diesel fuel and sawdust. But I truly love cutting, so much so that I do it not only to heat our home but also to avoid doing pretty much anything else I ought to be doing instead. The expansive woodpiles strewn along the half-mile-long driveway up to Ranting Hill make plain how wonderfully I have succeeded in using cutting to evade the pesky, endless round of adult responsibilities.

In addition to offering an escape from the scurrying of grown-up life, woodcutting also has the advantage of being ridiculously gear intensive. It isn't just the pickup truck, dump trailer, chainsaws, bars, chains, gas, oil, screnches, wedges, field axes, and files but also the stylish safety apparel. To begin with, there is the standard-issue, head-to-toe Carhartt in the classic, monkey-poop brown. I have graduated from ordinary work gloves to gel-palmed chainsaw gloves, with wraparound Velcro wrist straps; whenever I put them on, I feel like I am about to win the Indy 500. I have also traded in my steel-toed work boots for titanium-toed boots, which provide the same protection but are lighter and, more important, sound cool. I'm now considering "Titanium Toed" (or "Titanium Toad"?) for the name of my next band.

In the area of eye protection, I have improved my look over time, from the boxy, safety goggles of a high-school chemistry student to the reflector shades of an undercover cop to the tinted wraparounds of the professional bass fisherman. My final step has been to go for the full headgear: a bright orange hard hat, with attached ear protection and stylish nylon mesh visor, which makes me look like a blaze orange medieval knight. Whenever I am wearing this helmet, I am transformed into Sir Rantsalot, the brave, saw wielding knight-errant who can flip his visor up and deliver a cool, witty line every time. Unfortunately, I sometimes forget that I have the fancy headgear on and spit heartily without first raising the visor, a very gross bush-league move that I try to hide from anyone who might be in a position to comment on my mistake.

But the pièce de résistance of any chainsawing getup must be the chaps. You can't help but feel studly as a bronc buster once you have strapped these bad boys on, and I speak from experience when I say that being wrapped in Kevlar is a good idea when wielding a tool with razor-sharp teeth that are moving inches from your body at ninety feet per second (around sixty miles per hour). That manly valorization notwithstanding, it is a plain fact that chaps are essentially assless pants.

Several years ago, on Christmas Eve, Eryn let slip that Santa had brought me a new pair of chaps. (I had nicked the old ones, which, like a climbing rope that has sustained a fall, may have saved your life but should not be reused.) I was so excited that I snuck to the Christmas tree later that night—wearing only green, elf-themed boxer shorts—just to try on the new gear. The chaps fit so perfectly that I decided to treat myself to a celebratory nightcap. I was bent over, reaching into the fridge for a Black Butte porter, when I heard someone behind me. I spun around to see my father-in-law, who was then visiting from California for the holidays. This guy is an ex-cop, and he has always seemed to me like he is eight feet tall. There he stood, towering silently over me. I had to think fast, so I opened the beer, extended it toward him, and said, "Remember how you felled a tree in the wrong direction and knocked out power to half of Oakland during a Raiders game? I won't mention that, if you won't mention this." He took the beer and went back to bed with nothing more said, either then or since.

I do most of my woodcutting with my buddy Steve, who is so good with a saw that when we cut together I call him "the good feller." He just refers to me as "the other feller." Steve will take on trees twice the size I am willing to wrangle, and he'll do it even in rough terrain or in situations where the drop must be perfect. Before Steve fells a tree, he engages in a mysterious, elaborate ritual that appears entirely unscientific. He first breaks a branch, measures it against the length of his arm, and then backs away from the tree that is to be cut, holding the branch up in the air like a witch doctor and squinting at it with his head cocked to one side like a parrot. Then, he stares around the canopy of the forest, as if searching for celestial signs. After this period of inscrutable meditation, he sticks the branch into the ground and pronounces calmly that this is the exact spot where the tip of the tree's crown will strike on the drop. This is a little like Babe Ruth pointing to the spot in the bleachers where he will smack the dinger, and about as difficult to make good on.

Once Steve begins to wedge the bole and then notch the hinge—which, on a big tree, he does using a massive Stihl with a forty-two-inch bar (take a moment to visualize this)—it is impossible not to admire the guy's sheer gumption. And when he cuts the engine on his saw and begins driving wedges into the notch with the head of his field axe, that is my cue to spring into action. I coolly raise the visor on my helmet, spit heartily, and holler, "I'm here for you if you need anything, buddy!" Then I hastily retreat, until I am about a quarter-mile from the tree, perfectly safe and of no possible use to anyone save my bartender, who cannot afford to lose me. Steve's hammering echoes through the forest and is followed by the slow-motion sound of the holding wood cracking, the tree crashing through the canopy, and the resounding thud as it meets the earth—a heavy vibration that I feel in the titanium toes of my boots, despite my cowardly distance from the site. Reapproaching, I inevitably find that the tree has been dropped on a dime, with Steve's stick marking accurately the crown's position on the ground.

In addition to tackling trees well over 100 feet tall, including dead giants that threaten to destroy buildings were they to become windfall or be felled imprecisely, Steve is also capable of making beautiful objects with them once they are on the ground. Using his Alaska mill, a portable frame that guides a chainsaw, allowing its bar to move smoothly while cross-sectioning a length of log, he creates immense slabs that he later crafts into a variety of lovely things. The entry hall of our home on Ranting Hill is graced by a gorgeous bench that Steve fashioned from part of an eighty-five-foot-tall incense cedar that he felled. The bench is six feet long, but the entire piece is crafted from the same slab, so the grain wraps beautifully from the bench's surface around to its legs.

I have been a dedicated environmentalist for more than three decades, but it is my experience that fellow enviros are not always warm to my passion for woodcutting. I do understand that, intuitively, my hobby might appear to be the opposite of tree hugging, especially to folks who hold the reasonable view that we humans should quit messing with nature and just let it do its thing. But the problem is that one of the things nature does extremely well is burn stuff down, which has prompted massive fire suppression efforts along the Sierra front—efforts that have led to forests that are unnaturally dense, combustible, and vulnerable to die-off caused by the stress of drought and beetle kill. When John Muir wrote of walking through park-like Sierra forests reminiscent of a cathedral, he was describing an open, fire-scoured landscape that no longer exists in most parts of this range.

The trees I cut are already dead, and even then I am careful not to fell all standing dead trees in an area, leaving for wildlife habitat at least the number of snags per acre recommended by conservation biologists. I also try to cut in a way that mimics the thinning effects of a low-intensity ground fire, removing ladder saplings, jackstrawed ground fuels, and trees that have fallen victim to invasion by beetles. In doing so, I not only try to make a patch of forest a bit more like it would have been under a natural fire regime; I also use the environmentalist tool of the chainsaw to help create a forest that is a little less likely to be incinerated by the kind of catastrophic, stand-replacing canopy fire that can occur in areas where fire suppression has caused fuel densities to become unnaturally extreme.

The dead and downed wood I cut *will* burn, but in our wood-stove rather than in the forest, which raises the question, "Is heating with wood an environmentally responsible choice?" As with most good questions, the answer to this one is, "It depends." In many parts of the world, the unsustainable overharvesting of fuelwood is decimating forests, but that is certainly not the case in the eastern Sierra. In many instances, wood is burned in stoves that are inefficient; however, we use an extraordinarily effective appliance that employs a catalytic converter and emits less than three grams of particulate per hour. Even this tiny amount of particulate means that wood burning is generally not a good choice in urban settings, a concern that does not apply here in this remote, sparsely populated desert. In some circumstances, wood is burned to heat houses that are thermally inefficient, but our passive-solar home is so capable of capturing and holding heat that we burn approximately half the wood that would be needed in a conventionally designed home. If one burns sustainably harvested, well-seasoned wood in a properly sized, EPA-certified stove, this form of heating has a lot to recommend it.

But, my fellow enviros persist, "Doesn't the gasoline burned in trucks and chainsaws mean that woodcutting depends upon fossil fuels and thus contributes to CO_2 emissions?" The long answer is, "Yes, but each BTU of fossil fuel consumed to harvest wood produces twenty-five BTUs of heat, which is an impressive ratio. And, given that the trees I cut are already dead and that the carbon sequestered in them will be released into the atmosphere through controlled burn, wildfire, or rotting, the fact that the wood's combustion occurs in my stove limits both greenhouse gas emissions and the open release of particulate pollutants, not to mention that it also warms my family."

The real question is not whether burning wood is carbon neutral and zero emission but whether it is better than the alternatives practically available to me. I could heat with oil or gas, whose extraction and combustion are major contributors to the global climate change crisis; or, I could choose electricity, knowing that half of the megawatts produced in the United States are generated by burning coal, which is no improvement. Once active solar is within our financial reach, that will be our choice. In the meantime, I would rather harvest the BTUs I need with my own hands from the beautiful tinderbox of a Sierra forest than buy them from an oil rig in the Gulf of Mexico, a fracking well in North Dakota, or an open-pit coal mine in Wyoming.

The greatest pleasure offered by my woodcutting occurs around the hearth, which is the center of our home up on Ranting Hill. Here, my family gathers to enjoy each other's company and to savor that deeply satisfying, bone-warming radiant heat that is unique to wood. It is amazing how often, while adding fuel to the stove, I will recognize an individual log and remember its small story: not only what species of tree but precisely where it stood or fell, if it was snowing or shining the day I hauled it back to the desert, whether I bucked it from the trunk of a tree surgically dropped by that good feller, Steve.

A Zen proverb offers this guidance: "Before enlightenment, chop wood, carry water. After enlightenment, chop wood, carry water." There is something nourishing and elemental in this harvest. Gathering this wood from the high Sierra has warmed me more than twice, for, in addition to warming me through work and by fire, it has kindled my imagination in a way that no turning of a thermostat dial ever could.

ROAD CAPTAIN

I RECENTLY RECEIVED a phone call with the bad news that I have been given what my neighbors here in Silver Hills refer to as a "redneck promotion." I have been promoted from plain member and citizen to Road Captain, which is a position no sensible person would covet. Despite the cool title and apparently elevated rank, the job is without compensation or administrative support, is unelected, and descends upon you by fiat when the current Road Captain declares that you are it.

The road to Ranting Hill is 2.3 miles long and has eight houses scattered along it. It is a terrible road that degenerates to pure caliche mud in winter and bone-rattling, dust-choked washboard in summer. There have been times when it was so dry and abused as to be barren of gravel; at other times, it has been impassible because flash floodwaters flowed across it in an unbroken sheet. Many seasons it is so muddy that we Silver Hillbillies must resort to hanging around in town drinking beer after work just to kill enough time for the mud to freeze up so we can cross it to reach our homes.

The road's ditches are full of silt, what few culverts there are have crushed heads, and if there were ever any road signs they have long since blown away in the Washoe Zephyr or been hung on a horseshoe nail in somebody's pole barn. (Our mailboxes are all crooked, and our addresses are out of numerical order, too, but that's another story.) This is a private road, which means that, while the county will not maintain it, no one else wants to either. So who, by default, is in charge of stewarding this mess? The Road Captain.

Many years ago, we had a neighborhood association out here, to which we paid modest annual dues that were used only for road work and snow removal. Since most Silver Hillbillies are by nature unsociable, misanthropic, and share a worldview that tilts toward conspiracy theories and radical libertarianism, an overwhelming majority of my neighbors voted to rid themselves of the association—in the spirit of oppressed peasants ousting an occupying foreign army. The theory seemed to be that anyone who would collect association dues would soon come for our shotguns, bird dogs, and sour mash.

Since the demise of the association our bad roads have become worse, and some roads have descended into social chaos. On one nearby road that has only four houses, each neighbor has adopted the same strategy of trying to outwait the other three to see who will find the road so intolerable that they give in and fix it themselves. So far, nobody has relented, even when, for weeks at a time, they were all forced by deep mud to park at the paved road and slog the long haul up to their homes. On another road, a guy who is especially entrepreneurial bought an expensive grader in hopes he would have a field day. But, because he was once seen meeting with our local real estate developer, nobody would hire him, and, before long, the bank repossessed his shiny grader. On a third road, a guy who had repaired the roadbed at his own expense threatened to install a toll gate if his skinflint neighbors would not pony up their share.

On our road, this sort of chaos was averted through the leadership of my friend Ludde, a seventy-year-old man who lives on seventy acres across the draw from Ranting Hill. He is, hands down, the toughest and most curmudgeonly guy I have ever met, which is another way of saying that he is my role model and hero. For many years now Ludde has been our Road Captain, and it is a role that suits him perfectly. He does not speak often, but when he does everyone pays attention. For example, while riding his big stallion out in the desert he is fond of mentioning to illegal off-roaders, wherever he finds them, that "this is my favorite place to shoot, because I'd never expect anybody to be riding here. Why, a fella could get himself killed." You'd fear this guy even if he did not carry a twelve-gauge in a saddle scabbard by his right shin, which he does.

On another occasion, Ludde confronted a dirt biker who was shredding our road. The biker, who did not realize who he was talking to, cussed the old man out and tore off. Ludde climbed into his huge, white F-350 pickup and chased the motorcyclist for several miles along BLM roads at high speed, until the biker laid it down on a loose turn. Ludde left his truck idling and walked slowly up to the young man, who lay sprawled near his wrecked bike with a broken arm. Looking down with a warm smile, Ludde said, "Looks like your arm is bent funny, partner. Well, nice day for a walk." With that, he cocked his buckaroo hat, climbed back into his rig, and drove contentedly home.

It takes that kind of grit to be an effective Road Captain. One time, a neighbor on the road to the south of us went rogue and drove overland across her property and some public land to use our road, because her own had become impassable. On the day the lady pioneered this route, Ludde intercepted her and explained that if she wanted to use our road she was welcome to, but she'd have to pay the same amount the rest of us do to keep it up. The woman not only refused but produced a .30-06 deer rifle, which she gripped while responding that she'd do as she pleased. Ludde didn't blink. Walking slowly away, he said only, "We all pitched in and bought a little rock for the road. Let me know by morning if you decide to pay your share." The next morning, Ludde had two end dump truck loads of road base deposited directly in the mouth of the makeshift driveway the woman had been using to access our road. I will spare you the math: this is a quarter of a million pounds of gravel. Ludde left that monster pile there until the woman learned what the rest of us already knew: you don't mess with our Road Captain.

To be such a tough guy, Ludde is also good-humored, supportive, and flexible. Whenever a neighbor could not afford to pay their fair share, he would cover them until their cash flow improved. Once, he let a neighbor work off his road dues doing roofing work on Ludde's barn, after which Ludde paid the man's share. Another neighbor who has a big tractor contributes his share by doing ditching work along the road. Yet another never pays American dollars but always produces two loads of "rock" (shorthand for type-two road base gravel), which is a meaningful contribution, even though no money changes hands. Ludde understands that rock is the coin of the realm out here—a kind of redneck Bitcoin—and that it can be traded for almost anything. A neighborly swap might involve farrier tools, a case of whiskey, a calf, or a truck winch, and that is fine with Ludde, so long as the exchange ends in the common currency of rock, which then goes down on our road.

When I answered the phone yesterday evening, Ludde's first words were, "I've got some good news for you, partner."

"Let me guess. You didn't shoot anybody today?" I replied.

"I've already told everybody else on the road," he continued, ignoring me. "And more good news: this redneck promotion comes with a six-pack. Congratulations."

"Ludde, please tell me this isn't what I think it is. *Please*. What have I ever done to you? Haven't I been a good neighbor all these years?" I asked.

"Yup. That's why I have confidence in you, Captain," he replied, only emphasizing the word *captain* a little.

"Listen," I pleaded. "You were *born* to do this job. I don't have the cojones to run this road. Why in hell would you want me?"

"Because you're fair. Not very tough, but fair. And you're one of the only folks on the road who hasn't been threatened with a gun," Ludde explained.

"Yeah, but that'll change as soon as I'm Captain. These Silver Hillbillies will eat me alive."

"Comes with the territory, son. Besides, this isn't noggin surgery. What did I do when old lady Jenkins said we should reckon each person's dues by their distance from the paved road?" he asked.

"Nothing?" I guessed.

"How about when Matt wanted to figure dues by how many vehicles each family drives?"

"Not a thing," I answered.

"And when Smitty complained about the weight of Roper's flatbed? Or when Bill said he wouldn't pay up until Janie did? Or when Jesse put buckshot into the side of the FedEx truck, because it was going too fast?"

"Nothing," I repeated. "Not a damned thing."

"Got the picture, Captain? Everybody pays the same amount, due at the same time, unless they make a swap or show up with rock. Simple."

"I really don't want to do this, Ludde, but you leave me no choice. Can I, at least, call on you for help when things get rough?"

"Nope," he replied. "Now, you go share this good news with Hannah and Caroline. It isn't every little girl has a daddy who's a Road Captain. And drop by for that six-pack anytime."

MY FIRST RODEO

MY BUDDY TONY, who is also a licensed athletic trainer, fixes broken cowboys. Traveling from town to town, rodeo to rodeo, his job is to provide emergency medical aid and physical therapy to the young men and women athletes who are thrown by horses, kicked by bulls, or otherwise injured in a sport the *L.A. Times* reports is ten times more dangerous than football and thirteen times more hazardous than ice hockey. As an athletic trainer, Tony is specifically educated in sports medicine injuries, rehabilitation, and trauma triage. He has been in the business for almost forty years, and it is not unusual for him to treat cowboys whose fathers he treated back in their own rodeo days.

"Mostly small stuff this weekend," Tony said casually, as he worked expertly on my lower back. "In team roping, a cowboy got snared up and it yanked his thumb off. Tried to sew it back on, but it didn't take. Similar thing happened to a chute boss a couple weeks ago. That one was just the tip of the finger though. Took us awhile to find it. Put it in a saline bag and gave it to him to take with him to the ER. Not sure how that one turned out."

"Man, Tony, that sounds brutal," I replied, cringing as I flexed my fingers.

"That's nothing. A month back, a cowboy got stomped by a real big bull, so I went in to help him. I'd just got his head and neck immobilized in my hands when that bull turned and charged me," explained Tony, in an oddly calm tone of voice.

"Damn, what did you do?" I asked, sitting up for a reply.

"Nothing you *can* do. Spinal injury. Can't let the kid's head go. Clown got the bull's attention and the bullfighter veered him off at the last second, so it all worked out. Got the cowboy on a back-board. Unconscious, but he came to later," Tony said, in the same unaccountably cool tone.

Six weeks later, Tony has arranged for a press pass allowing me to attend my first rodeo: the Reno Rodeo, which is advertised as "The Wildest, Richest Rodeo in the West," and where more than a half-million bucks of prize money will be won. I arrive at the live-stock events center early and wander through a dizzying labyrinth of concessions. Bridle and saddle outfits are numerous under the big tent, as are stands selling beautiful Mexican blankets, colorful beadwork, and finely crafted turquoise and silver Navajo jewelry. There are fringed buckskin jackets and delicately braided lanyards and big silver belt buckles. The smell of dust and leather is in the air. A woman is being fitted for spangled chaps in one booth; in another, an older man is airbrushing pastel coyotes onto the foam faces of trucker caps. Nearby, a sign reads, "Horsehair belts made in America, not in mainland communist China."

A young woman walks by in sequin-encrusted jeans and a tight tank top emblazoned with the slogan "Huntin' and Lovin.'" She heads into a makeshift cantina where a country band is belting out a ballad that includes the memorable line "Tennessee whiskey got me drinking in heaven." Centered above the louvered, swinging saloon doors is a large oil painting depicting George Washington, American flag in hand, heroically crossing the Delaware. At first glance, the patriotic image resembles Emanuel Leutze's famous 1851 painting of the scene, until I look again and notice that the father of our country is tricked out in full cowboy regalia, from buckaroo hat to batwing chaps to stylishly tooled leather boots.

Having been forewarned that even with my press pass I won't be permitted behind the chutes unless I'm wearing boots, jeans, a western shirt, and a cowboy hat, I've done my best to cobble together an acceptable uniform—though a quick glance around this place makes it clear that I've missed the mark. My jeans are Levi's instead of Wrangler, my shirt has buttons rather than snaps, and my boots are pointed-toe instead of being square-toed ropers. My belt buckle is laughably puny. I don't even own a cowboy hat, so the next order of business is to acquire this indispensable part of my costume before the event begins. I settle on an inexpensive, black felt cowboy hat that is steamed and fitted to my noggin by a woman who smiles politely at the fact that I'm so obviously out of my element. It likely wouldn't matter if I were the best-outfitted fake cowboy in Reno, because I'm busy recording my observations in a leather-bound journal. Nothing will out you faster in any alien social environment than writing—a gesture that amounts to a public confession that you are a cultural anthropologist and not a member of the tribe.

Soon enough I find Tony, whose home away from home is the forty-foot-long, fully-outfitted sports medicine trailer sponsored by the Justin Boot Company. Stepping up into the trailer I'm suddenly immersed in a welter of cowboys and a nearly equal number of athletic trainers, hurrying sideways past each other in the trailer's narrow aisle as they come and go, receiving and giving treatment before the event begins. The cowboys and cowgirls look incredibly fit and strong, and they are surprisingly young. I've been told that in several rodeo events, twenty-three passes for old, and as I glance at the injuries being treated here I begin to sense why. While there are plenty of stitches and scars in view—not to mention eggplant-colored bruises, swollen knees and ankles, and cowboys so thoroughly taped up that they look like aspiring mummies—it is also evident that many of these athletes suffer from head, shoulder, neck, and spine injuries.

The cowboys all seem to know each other, and although they will soon be in fierce competition, they are friendly and sociable in the trailer. The liveliest of the young men being worked on is the rodeo clown, an energetic, charismatic, irresistibly droll kid who is already sporting full makeup. His clown smile, which is painted on, does not obscure the genuine smile beneath it. "Rather not say what I get paid to live or die in that barrel," he says with a wide grin, referring to the essential prop that is often the only object standing between his fragile body and the hulking mass of the bull. "Don't mind the rolling so much, but that bull flipped me twice last night," the clown continues buoyantly, rubbing his neck and grinning. "Tonight I think I'll just relax in there until the show's over," he says, to no one in particular. "Not a bad little roundhouse I've got. Keeps me out of the rain. Rent's cheap. Gettin' so it feels like home to me now," he continues, now flirting with a barrel racer who is receiving knee work. "Room for two, cowgirl. You ever seen my barrel? Come by after bulls, and I'll show you around in there. Nice and cozy!" Everyone laughs, including the girl.

Spirited banter is clearly part of the culture of this community of athletes, but the clown may also be warming up his public persona. His fascinating and important job is to protect bucked cowboys from enraged mustangs and bulls by helping to distract the animal while the so-called bullfighters work to distract the bull from the fallen rider. The clown uses his barrel strategically, as an island of safety for himself and the bullfighters. But not only that—the clown must execute remarkable feats of athleticism and courage while also somehow making the audience laugh. Only a special combination of agility, strength, and speed allows him to protect the riders—as well as the bullfighters and himself—from being kicked, stomped, or gored. That comedy is part of his charge seems an extravagant demand, but one that may be as necessary as it is required. By smiling his double smile in the face of death, the clown convinces the gasping spectators that, however difficult it might seem, it is possible to face fear with humor. It is a perilous job—the clown's courage and his foolishness are the two sides of a thin coin that must be flipped and made to land on its edge.

As event time approached, the cowboys thinned out, giving me a chance to talk with Tony and the other athletic trainers and emergency medical staff in the trailer. They are genuinely nice folks, serious about their craft, and honestly concerned for the well-being of the rodeo competitors. It is also clear they must accept that there is only so much they can do to help.

"Everybody out there rides hurt," Tony explained, nodding toward the arena. "This isn't basketball or baseball, where if you're injured you surf the bench while you heal. To win, these guys have to ride. If they miss events, they don't earn prize money, and if they don't earn, they've got no shot at the national championships in Vegas. We patch them up the best we can, but when we see them in a week at the next rodeo, they're gonna be out there riding again, hurt or not. That cumulative trauma is real hard, especially on muscle tears and concussions."

Although the rodeo was now in full swing, Tony explained that we'd be going out to the arena only for the events most likely to result in injury: saddle bronc and bulls. Once the steer wrestling and team roping events had concluded without serious harm to the competitors, we made our way through grandstand security until we stood immediately behind the chutes in anticipation of the saddle bronc competition. From this vantage point, just feet away from the action, the physical intensity of the event was palpable. The sheer power and muscular strength of the horse became obvious when it began to resist its confinement in the chute. Rather than taking wildness out of the animal, as Old West bronc busters once did, wildness had been put into these animals, which are carefully bred and selected for their desperate resistance to human mastery.

The first bronc was wrangled into its chute and mounted by a short, solid cowboy, who worked hard to get astride the animal and keep from having his legs crushed between the horse's flanks and the surrounding chute rails. The cowboy wore a padded safety vest spangled with sponsor patches, but no other protective gear. His arms were completely wrapped in athletic tape. He struggled to achieve a fiercely tight grip, which is an absolute necessity in this sport, because during the ensuing adventure, the cowboy has only his one-handed grasp of a simple rein to prevent him from being launched. Once in position on the horse with his fist bolted to the rein, the stout cowboy used his free hand to slap himself repeatedly in the face in hopes of releasing a bracing rush of adrenaline that would help prepare him for the much greater rush that was about to come.

When the gate swung open, that bronc exploded out of the chute with the speed and power of lightning released from a bottle—bucking, diving, and spinning all at once, the cowboy pitching forward and back in a wild motion that looked as if it could in a matter of seconds destroy a spine for life. The bronc bucked so violently that when the rider's hat came off it shot straight up into the air a dozen feet or so, giving a clear indication of the sheer vertical force produced by the bucking. The centrifugal force of the bronc's simultaneous spinning was made evident in the next second, when the cowboy did not fall from the horse but rather flew sideways from it, as if shot from a cannon.

This scene was repeated, with few of the cowboys remaining aboard the whirling broncs for more than a few seconds, but each of them riding with a rhythm and beauty that even an uninitiated spectator could easily appreciate. As the young men were tossed, one by one, into the arena dust, I was amazed that every one of them managed to stand up and walk away under their own power—though several did so slowly, and one had an obvious limp. At one point, a cowboy who had been violently pitched took a long time getting to his feet. I asked Tony if he was going to help the kid. "Cowboy code," he replied, without looking over at me. "Have to let him walk out if he can. I go in for him now, he'd never trust me to work on him again." The young man tottered out of the arena, and then pulled himself unsteadily into the medical trailer. I would later see him, perfectly cheerful, with stitches holding tight a fresh laceration on his forehead.

With the conclusion of the saddle bronc competition we returned to the trailer, where Tony worked on a few more injured athletes while the tie-down roping and barrel racing events continued apace. On the small, closed-circuit television monitor inside the trailer I could see—during a break in more serious action—the "mutton busting" spectacle, a comic interlude in which young kids hold tightly to the backs of sheep, which are then released to run the arena until the kids, unable to hang on any longer, fall into the same dust where the pitched bronc riders had lately sprawled.

At last, it was time for the final event of the rodeo, and I didn't have to understand anything about it to sense its importance. The large crowd became discernibly more boisterous, nervous, and agitated. The trailer suddenly emptied of medical personnel, who followed Tony in a direct march to the arena, where they stationed themselves along the corral rails with an intensity not noticeable during earlier events. The sense of some finale was in the air.

Although bull taming spectacles date back to ancient Greece, modern bull riding evolved from Mexican *charreada*, contests of ranch skills and prowess that, by the sixteenth century, had come to include a bull riding contest called the *jaripeo*. During the mid-nineteenth century, bull riding became increasingly common in Texas and other borderlands areas where Hispanic and Anglo ranchers worked together in small, rural communities. Competitive bull riding as it exists today emerged during the Great Depression, when the milder-mannered steers (castrated bulls) then used in rodeos were replaced with brahma bulls and their crossbreeds—powerful, aggressive animals that wield deadly horns, can weigh upward of 2,000 pounds, and display testosterone-fueled rage at every turn. It was these fierce brahma bulls that the hopeful young cowboys at the Reno Rodeo were about to mount and attempt to ride.

Bull riding has been called "the most dangerous eight seconds in sports," because that is the length of time a rider—who must hold on with only one hand to the braided bull rope, which is strapped around the bull's chest—is required to remain astride the animal in order to qualify to be scored on the quality of his ride. Riders have been severely injured and even killed by bulls who have kicked, trampled, or gored them. Also at severe risk of injury are the rodeo clowns and bullfighters, whose job it is to remain near the bull and to distract the beast when the rider is thrown and would otherwise be entirely vulnerable. Clowns and bullfighters have also been killed, often while trying to protect a fallen rider from a furious bull, and occasionally while attempting to free a rider who had become "hung up" in the bull rope—or even entangled in the bull's horns—a potentially fatal predicament for both the cowboy and those whose job it is to protect him.

As I watched the first of the bulls being prodded into the chute just a few yards away from me, I was taken aback by the sheer bulk of the animal. While the saddle broncs had manifest grace and beauty in their demeanor, here I witnessed an animal of a very different sort. The bull seemed unspeakably primitive, as if it had been forged in some world other than and before our own. In the eye of the horse I detected some relation, a sense that behind that gleaming eye ticked the brain of a fellow mammal. No such kinship was visible in the small, black eyes of the hulking bull.

The cowboy who was to ride this first bull strode past me confidently and then clambered along the top of the chute until he straddled the rails above the bull. From there he lowered himself gently onto the animal's broad, black back. There followed a good deal of commotion, as the bull pushed and tried to buck, the chute boss and his crew worked to restrain the animal, and the cowboy struggled to secure his firm, one-handed grip on the rope. The rodeo clown and bullfighters positioned themselves strategically in the arena. At last, after one final, breathless moment of calm, the gate swung open and the bull blasted out of its confinement, tearing into the arena while bucking forward and backward and spinning at the same time. It seemed impossible that an animal so immense could kick, rear, and twist with such agility and force, and twice it bucked into the air and twisted so violently while airborne as to perform a full 180-degree spin before thundering back to earth. Watching the cowboy desperately holding on to that giant bolt of black lightning, I understood for the first time that eight seconds is a very, very long time.

This spectacular performance was repeated, as cowboy after cowboy tried their best to reach eight seconds astride the backs of the giant, flying, twisting, 1,800- or 2,000-pound animals. Most failed. For their part, the bulls appeared so primeval as to seem antediluvian—as if each cowboy might just as well have been riding an angry triceratops or stegosaurus, or even astride some dark creature born of imagination or nightmare. But what struck me most throughout this event was not the huge bulls, or even the flying cowboys. It was instead the clown. Here was a young man dressed to play the fool in his flowing costume of bright, motley colors, bringing comedy to a scene that threatened at any moment to result in serious injury to those around him or to himself.

I gazed in admiration as the clown thrilled the crowd with his antics. He appeared as agile as a gymnast, as fast as a sprinter, as quick as a prize fighter. At times he taunted the bulls, turning his back on them and strolling away, daring them, through pantomime, to render him a parti-colored shish kebab. Standing behind his protective barrel, he would roll it audaciously toward a bull to provoke a response. At other moments, he climbed inside the protective device, from which emerged a single arm, waving a cowboy hat to invite the bull to hammer the barrel. Or, he would pop his head out just long enough to plant his thumbs on his ears and waggle his fingers derisively toward the bull before again disappearing from view. The laughter he elicited from the crowd seemed partly a response to his farce and partly a release of the nervous tension produced by our uncertainty about his ultimate safety.

If the clown's art consisted of a provocative combination of daring and absurdity, the peak of his performance was his willingness to literally run circles around the bull—its wheeling horns just a foot or so behind the arch of his back—as injured cowboys were hustled out of the arena before they could be attacked by the angry bull that had just ejected them. As a spectator, I found these moments difficult to process; they were clearly the most dangerous, and yet also the funniest. There was a Chaplinesque quality to the clown, as if, though in constant danger, this jester possessed the cartoon character's magical powers of resilience and even immortality. The closer the bull came to goring the clown, the more I laughed; but the more I laughed, the more I found myself laughing through a disconcerting feeling that amusement was the wrong response to the actions of a man who was operating within inches of his life. Perhaps the clown understood that it is his natural work to keep the forces of comedy and tragedy in close relation to one another. Humorists always do their best work close to the bull.

After the rodeo, I followed Tony back to the medical trailer, where I returned to writing in my field journal while he and his crew resumed fixing broken cowboys. A few moments later the door burst open and the clown, still in full costume and makeup, jumped into the trailer. He beelined for the freezer and reached deeply into it, presumably to bag some ice to treat a fresh injury.

"That bull tag you?" asked one of the Justin sports medicine athletic trainers, with some concern.

"No, sir!" said the clown in a burst of enthusiasm, as he pulled out and cracked open a tallboy can of beer he had hidden beneath the cubes. Everyone chuckled.

As he turned to leave, beer in hand, the clown noticed me scribbling in my journal.

"You a preacher?" he asked earnestly.

"Nope, but I can sermonize in a pinch," I replied, smiling.

"Not tonight, Parson; these folks have suffered enough!" he declared loudly, as everyone laughed together again.

"*Paint Your Wagon*," I returned, recognizing that old film as the source of his perfectly timed joke.

"Well, preacher," he said, grinning through his painted-on smile and reaching out his hardened hand to shake mine, "I might just join your congregation." And with that, he bolted for the trailer door.

"Take care of yourself," I said, as he left.

"My mother prays for me," he replied as he swung himself out the door, "so I'll be allright."

IH8 DMV

I HAVE ALWAYS been entertained by vanity license plates—at least when they are genuinely clever or funny—and have long thought that a little back bumper wit on my part might help my fellow Silver Hillbillies endure the one stoplight that interrupts our twenty-five-mile cruise from here to town. But there are perfectly good reasons why I have never made a move on customized plates. First, I am so frugal as to have trouble rationalizing an unnecessary expense. Second, I like to change my mind about things and so have been hesitant to commit to one message, however witty or insightful. Most important, to get customized plates I would have to go to the Department of Motor Vehicles, a place that is the seventh circle of administrative hell, even in a Kafkaesque world already overflowing with mind-numbing bureaucratic horseshit. I just have not thought of a vanity plate funny enough to make it worth the misery of wasting hours at the DMV.

That did not keep me from thinking about the possibility of custom tags, and, occasionally I would toy with ideas. I reckoned I would go with something that would assert my identity as a high desert hillbilly, like DSRT RAT or BSN RNGE or GR8 BSN or DSRT MTN. Even something Boulderesque like NEWWEST could be cool. Or I might go with a wiser, place-based proclamation like IM SAGE. Or maybe I could tap the nickname we sometimes use for rattlers out here: BZZZWRM. It also occurred to me that I could cleverly use the fact that our state tags boldly say NEVADA atop them to create a two-word slogan by adding NOTWSTLD, since "Nevada: Not a Wasteland" is the slogan used by those of us who would just as soon not have the nation's high-level nuclear waste buried in our home state. Another two-word message could be produced by choosing WD OPN, since one of our many equivocal state mottoes is "Nevada: Wide Open," a slogan that seems vaguely to refer not only to landscapes but also to booze and pot laws, accelerators, and thighs.

While I was dreaming up customized Nevada tags I came up with other ideas that might work for someone else in Silver Hills, if not for me. One of my neighbors, who is a professional poker player, might either DBL DWN or FOLDEM. The old lady at the only gas station in our valley likes to pull slots, so she could hope to HIT 37S, while her friend, who plays roulette, could choose RDR BLK. The guy up the road from us raises longhorns and so might like to proclaim that he has BIG BLLS. Or maybe not. But he could still use STEERNG. My friend who paints desert landscapes should use RBBT BRSH, and Chickenfeathers, our neighborhood dowser, could declare HRS H2O. All the equestrians out here can argue over BITBYBIT, and the lady mining engineer might confess to being a GLD DGR. Mister Grumpledumps, our road's resident conspiracy theorist, should have CNA UFO. And our unreliable mail delivery woman, who has frosted blonde hair, poor taste in clothes, and a fancy tramp stamp lower back tattoo that reads "*LADY*," might do well to order up NTA HKR.

HOW TO CUSS IN WESTERN

I even resorted to going online to seek additional ideas for my would-be tag. There, I found a site called something like ZILLION-TAGS.COM, which not only featured many hundreds of actual vanity plates, but also had them organized by state, which I thought might help me determine where the good ideas were coming from. I began with my home state, which I soon discovered had mounted the most pathetic custom-tag display imaginable. Nevada had a total of four entries: IHVNOJB, 99 PROBS, IH8 WMPS, and the incredibly dumb NOT DUM.

Next, I turned to Utah, which provided no encouragement whatsoever. Utahans are apparently too well-mannered to excel at self-expression in the highly constrained rhetorical genre of the vanity plate. Like Nevada, Utah boasted only four entries, three of which I could not understand; the fourth was GOLFING, which struck me as genuinely depressing. Next I tried Idaho, which had a whopping five tags, not a single one of which made a lick of sense. Could these be survivalist code messages instructing rural neighbors to hoard guns and whiskey in anticipation of the apocalypse? In desperation I turned to Oregon, whose tags were weirdly sincere, like BEYRSLF and GOD NO1 and BE GR8R, though one lady, who reminded me of an old girlfriend, confessed to having PMS 247. Thankfully, I found that the Sand Cutters down in Arizona were more creative and had come through not only with many more tags but also with a variety of respectable entries, including AEIONU, SCO BEDO, VNTY PL8, MMMBEER, and RCY BOBY, not to mention the charmingly confessional IFARTED.

Although the plates of a few Arizonians were slightly risqué, like GETNAKD and IL SPNKU, they could not hold a candle to the work of my neighbors to the west. California had hundreds of custom-tag entries—many more than Nevada and all its other neighboring states combined. The messages on at least half the plates were pornographic, and even those that were not explicitly sexual seemed obsessed with power and money—a sentiment elegantly distilled by 2L8 11 on a new jag. But the California tags were also expressive, irreverent, and comical in ways that might prove instructive here in the desert West, where the plates were not only unimaginative, but frequently incomprehensible. Among the hundreds of solid entries from the Californicators were FROMMYX (on a Mercedes), MO FAUX (on a Caddy), JST 1MPG (on a Hummer), FRENDLY (on a creepy, windowless panel van), BLONDE (with the tag mounted upside down), GEEKDAD (on a Prius), H8LAFWY (on an old pickup), UGHHHH (on a Tercel), and my personal favorite: CMON WTF (on a yellow VW bug).

Despite all this inspiration, I still had not come up with anything clever enough to drive me to the dreaded DMV. But all that changed on my last birthday, when Eryn said she had made up my mind for me, adding that the deed was done and the plates were already ordered. She declined to tell me what my custom tags would proclaim, but she seemed confident I would appreciate the message. I had no alternative to being vocally appreciative and silently curious.

The state bureaucrats aged Eryn's paperwork as if it were a fine Pappy Van Winkle bourbon, but eventually we received word that my custom plates were available for pickup. I wondered if the new tags had been produced by inmates, as the "Live Free or Die" plates in New Hampshire reportedly are. It did occur to me that even the inmate of a federal penitentiary might hope to land in New Hampshire just to avoid having to make "Famous Potatoes" tags in Idaho, which might itself still be preferable to repeatedly stamping out a bad pun in Utah, where the goofy tags read "Greatest Snow on Earth!" Even if you like puns, it seems to me there's something ill-advised about choosing a tourism slogan that alludes to P. T. Barnum ("Greatest Show on Earth!"), the king of hucksters, a man who excelled at separating tourists from their money by never forgetting his core maxim that "Nobody ever lost a dollar by underestimating the taste of the American public."

Fetching my new slogan meant a trip to the DMV, a prospect that inspired unalloyed terror. This instinct was confirmed as I arrived at the facility, where the ironically inadequate parking had triggered a Darwinian battle for spaces, in which I was twice nearly sideswiped. Entering the building, I was directed to join a long line in order to get a number that would allow me to wait in another line that was much longer. After about forty minutes, I reached the front of this first line and was issued a number by a surly woman who was wearing a hair net, as if she worked not at the DMV but instead as a tater tot dolloper in a junior high school lunchroom. I then took a seat on one of the DMV chairs, torture devices that are bolted to the cinderblock walls and made of coarse wire mesh that invariably leaves a grid pattern on your butt, as if you've been whacked with an ass-sized flyswatter—though, in truth, the mesh may have been practical, given that several of my fellow citizens looked as if they might, at any moment, begin to urinate on themselves.

I say "my fellow citizens," because a visit to the DMV offers a spectacularly disturbing opportunity to witness what a cross-section of the local community actually looks like. On one side of me sat an older man who sounded as if he were negotiating an important business deal. Only later did I notice that he had no Bluetooth headset but was simply talking to himself. All the while his phone kept going off, and the ringtone was the unmistakable tune of Wild Cherry's midseventies hit, "Play That Funky Music White Boy." He never answered it.

The young man sitting on the other side of me had a weird tonsure haircut that looked as if someone had slapped a soup bowl on his noggin and shaved everything below the rim. He passed the time by loudly repeating every number as it was called by the

DMV's automated voice system. "Three hundred sixty-nine," droned the robot speaker, flatly. "Oh, *yeah*! That's *right*! Three hundred and *sixty-nine*!" yelled hair-tuft guy. "Three hundred seventy," said the soulless, mechanical voice. "Yeah, *baby*! There's three hundred and *seventy*! That's what I'm *talkin*'bout!" shouted the man. I looked down at my number and winced: 462. I had a long way to go.

Nearby, a lady was giving herself a full pedicure, complete with those little foam spacers that splayed her toes while the toxic fumes, perhaps mercifully, gave those of us around her a mild contact high. Another woman walked by wearing a puffy red parka and a plaid-green Elmer Fudd hunting cap with ear flaps dangling; below the waist, she wore only purple gym shorts and bright-orange flip flops. Babies were crying, and catatonic people were snoring, and a man who was apparently deaf was plucking a ukulele that was badly out of tune. Near a young couple, who were passing the time by making out, sat an angry-looking lady in a full clown suit who was herself sitting next to a young woman wearing a tight, bright yellow T-shirt advertising the famous Mustang Ranch brothel. No one seemed to notice the clown.

Blithe platitudes about democracy, equality, and respect for others are sorely tested at the DMV, where sustained exposure to my fellow citizens constantly threatened to drive me back to the exquisite remoteness of my desert home, from which I hoped never to return to town. I doubt that even Pete Seeger, may he rest in peace, could have endured more than an hour of this theater. DMV is the place where populist sentiment comes to die.

After the better part of two hours, the automated voice finally called my number. So numb was I that I did not notice, until I was startled to attention by hair-tuft guy, who shouted, "*No lie*, people! I'm preaching the *gospel* of four hundred and *sixty-two*!" Realizing, suddenly, that my number had been called, I jumped to my feet and waved it over my head as if I were a winning game-show contestant, before remembering that I had won nothing more than permission to take this excruciating experience to the next miserable step.

Feeling sheepish after my involuntary outburst, I slunk toward a phalanx of grumpy DMV minions, who sat behind a long counter that receded toward a vanishing point at the far end of the cavernous building. I walked up to the DMV lady who sat beneath the flashing number 462 and took a seat—wire mesh again, but it felt like a different grid pattern, which provided some relief for my cheeks, which were already molded to the texture of a waffle. I politely presented a folder that contained all the required documents: registration, smog check, proof of insurance, and receipt of payment for custom plates. The DMV lady sat motionless, staring at me with an expressionless face. She uttered not a single word.

"Um, OK," I stammered. "I'm here to pick up customized license plates. I have all the necessary paperwork."

She continued looking at me with an unblinking, reptilian stare. Even more surreal was the backdrop for her inexpressive countenance: on the wall behind her was a large poster featuring the smiling face of a pleasant looking woman above a morale-boosting motto that read, "I'm the DMV. Yes, I can help you with that!" I glanced down the long row of actual DMV people and saw not a single smile, either from them or from my fellow citizens, many of whom had been waiting for so many hours that they now struggled to utter a single word in any human language.

After a pause that seemed interminable, the lady rose stiffly from her chair and shuffled silently away like an overmedicated zombie. She may have gone to get my plates, but that was not at all clear, and after five minutes I began to wonder if she had simply gone on a cigarette break or maybe even left for the day. Or perhaps she just stepped into the mailroom to pour some bourbon into her coffee, a sensible measure that I regretted not having taken myself.

IH8 DMV

After about fifteen minutes, zombie lady shuffled back into view, mechanically reoccupying her place in front of me. Slowly extending her arm, she set a large, manila envelope on the counter between us. When she finally spoke, her entire discourse consisted of only two words, which were intoned as a question: "Ten bucks?"

I was confused. She had examined none of my paperwork, had explained nothing of the procedure, and now seemed to be inquiring whether I thought ten dollars was a reasonable price for whatever was in the envelope that now rested between us. I pulled out my wallet, plunked an Alexander Hamilton on the counter, and waited to see what might happen next. The lady slowly slid the manila envelope toward me across the counter, completing the motion by sweeping the ten spot toward herself, where she simply folded her hands over the bill. "Have a nice day," she said in an expressionless monotone.

It was not until I staggered back out into the light of day that I opened that envelope and pulled out what, to this day, remains the finest birthday gift I have ever received. Beneath the word "Nevada," the vanity plate read, in screaming all caps: RANTER.

The beauty of being a writer in love with humor is that everything in life that is not pleasure is still material, and in that sense my literary rantings have inoculated me against despair. In the life of a high desert Ranter, a good day becomes a memory, a bad day becomes a story, and even a visit to the DMV can have a happy ending. Still, even after a good laugh, IH8 DMV.

HOW TO CUSS IN WESTERN

DON'T FENCE ME IN

W HEN YOU LOOK at a fence, you are seeing something more than a material object. You are also seeing the embodiment of an idea—a form of symbolic communication that not only marks a boundary but also stakes a claim about the land and its uses. In feudal England most land remained in the "commons," shared fields where even peasants were allowed to practice subsistence agriculture. By the sixteenth century, however, wealthy landowners began to fence off the commons for their own benefit, dispossessing poor laborers and farmers and privatizing a natural resource that had long offered sustenance to the entire community. While we will never know who raised the first fence, Jean-Jacques Rousseau, a guy who thought harder about the social contract than I'm willing to, wrote that "The first man who, having fenced in a piece of land, said 'This is mine,' and found people naive enough to believe him, that man was the true founder of civil society." In establishing a new kind of relationship both with his neighbors and with the land, that first fence builder caused some problems we haven't yet solved.

Here in the American West we have long had a complicated relationship with fences. The "commons" of the frontier West was the open range that was utilized by wildlife, by Native American peoples, and, much later, by ranchers whose livelihood depended (and in many places still depends) upon the use of public lands. But legislation like the Homestead Act (1862) and the Desert Land Act (1877) granted legal possession of land to anyone who could "improve" it, and a fence was (and still is) considered an improvement to land. In other words, the fence functioned as the primary marker of possession and public assertion of ownership. The Range Wars of the nineteenth-century West were feuds over the right to fence off parts of this open range commons, particularly the parts that harbored the region's limited water sources. If skirmishes in those wars sometimes ended with six-guns, they usually began with barbed wire—a technology invented not long after the Civil War, and one that profoundly transformed the landscape of the West.

Beneath the politics and economics of the Range Wars is a different kind of conflict, one that is more a battle of ideas than one of land use. It is a war we're still fighting in the West today. Two of the strongest human impulses are the desire for home and the yearning for freedom, a pair of noble ideas that are sometimes at odds with each other. In erecting a fence between ourselves and the so-called "outside" world—a world that is rendered "outside" by the fence itself—we define and proclaim our home ground. In the parlance of the cultural geographer, the fence converts "space" into "place" by declaring the occupant's intention to separate a piece of land from the commons and stay put on it. Seen in this valorizing light, a fence encloses and protects a place that we care for, improve, nurture, and treasure. A fence communicates, both to ourselves and to our neighbors, an ennobling concept of home.

At the same time, we have always wanted the West to symbolize freedom, independence, and openness; we fantasize about it as a landscape in which we can be liberated from constraint. In the back of our minds, where we store the indelible images from old John Ford films, the West will always be a place that provides room to roam. To move "out" West from "back" East has long implied a movement from bondage into freedom, and nothing is so powerful a symbol of that emancipation as the sublime fenceless-ness of the iconic western landscape. This desire for liberty from constraint, which is expressed in so many western novels, films, and songs, is at the heart of the much-covered 1934 Cole Porter classic "Don't Fence Me In," which includes these lyrics:

I want to ride to the ridge where the West commences
And gaze at the moon till I lose my senses
And I can't look at hobbles and I can't stand fences
Don't fence me in

Like Porter's crooning cowboy, we Westerners "can't stand fences." How, then, are we to reconcile our celebration of open-ness and freedom with the fact that we have run an inconceivable amount of fence—that our region is in fact an immense, tightly latticed grid of mesh and wire? While hard numbers on fencing are difficult to come by, it has been estimated that the 350 million acres of western rangelands managed by the BLM and US Forest Service (USFS) contain over 100,000 miles of fence. Make that a five-strand fence, which it often is, and you have enough wire to get from anywhere in the West to the moon and back again (yes, literally). And this monstrous reckoning entirely omits fenc-ing on private lands. Does all this fence define our home, or limit our freedom? Does it protect us from the outside, or simply create more outside from which we then feel the need for protection?

Here on Ranting Hill I too have a complicated relationship with fences, one brought to my attention recently when a new neighbor on our rural road had his property fully fenced before moving in. He chose a six-strand wire fence, fifty-two inches high with a bottom strand just a few inches above the ground. I should add that this approach of immediately fencing one's property with five- or six-strand wire (usually barbed) is the default approach here in Silver Hills, and that in choosing to leave our property unfenced I am expressing a dissenting opinion on the subject. I have done so because we are close to public lands, and because our land is on pronghorn routes and mule deer winter range. "Oh, give me a home . . . where the deer and the antelope play." It is an old idea, and still a good one. One of the pleasures of sitting at my writing desk gazing out over our property is seeing pronghorn and deer move freely across the land. If they didn't, I might have to quit looking out the window and actually work.

The negative impact of these kinds of fences on wildlife is all too real. Although moose, bighorn sheep, elk, and deer can jump fences, fatal entanglement is disturbingly common, with studies suggesting that each year one ungulate ensnarement death occurs for every 2.5 miles of fence. And fences present significant barriers to pregnant and young animals. The same study indicated that when ungulates were found dead near (but not entangled in) fences, there was one annual death per 1.2 miles of fence. Ninety percent of these fatalities were fawns that were unable to cross the fence to follow their mothers. Multiply those casualty numbers by 100,000 miles of fence and that's a lot of carnage. Fences are also a serious hazard to birds such as swans, cranes, and geese, as well as the grouse, hawks, and owls that are native here in the sagebrush steppe.

Like all landowners, I have firm ideas about what I do and do not want on my property. Although I do want pronghorn and do not want off-road vehicles (ORVs), I have plenty of rural neighbors who don't care about wildlife but choose to live in this remote area precisely because they enjoy their ORVs; other neighbors value

HOW TO CUSS IN WESTERN

both ORVs and wild animals. But that's exactly my point. Each of us moved out here because we found town life too constraining, because we wanted to do what we damn well please with our own property and not have to conform to someone else's rules, or the values those rules codify. I am no different from my neighbors in this respect: I am here to indulge the fantasy that I can stake a claim to home without forfeiting my freedom in doing so.

It is a truism that you should never take down a fence until you first understand why it was put up. But around here most fences, which are both labor-intensive and expensive to build, aren't keeping much of anything either in or out. Technically this is open range, but there aren't many cattle on the public lands hereabouts, and in any case those few head mosey around on the other side of five barbed strands of BLM wire. With the exception of some practical horse fencing, the miles of wire that crisscross this swath of hilly high desert serve a mostly symbolic purpose. Just as it has for centuries, fencing in Silver Hills functions primarily as a proclamation of possession. Speaking as a guy who is especially fond of antelope, which have the most trouble navigating the kinds of fences we build out here, I believe that the loss of pronghorn on this land is too high a price to pay for a symbolic assertion of ownership.

Henry Thoreau once declared that "any man more right than his neighbors constitutes a majority of one already." The problem with Uncle Henry's bold assertion is that each of us is convinced that we are the one who is right. So let me back up a hitch and say not only that I recognize that some folks need fences but that I believe all folks should have them if they want them. I'm not after anybody's barbed wire, six-guns, or rights. So in the spirit of compromise I'd like to offer some practical suggestions for how we Westerners might have our fences—have them to fulfill all the real and symbolic purposes we want them to—and still radically reduce the slaughter of wildlife they currently cause. A few simple, cost-effective modifications can turn our fences from impenetrable death traps into navigable obstacles.

What I am about to tell you in this short paragraph summarizes the key findings from fence mortality research by wildlife biologists. Fences should be no higher than forty-two inches, a height above which some ungulates find jumping perilous. The distance between the top two wires should be at least twelve inches, because leg entanglement most often occurs between the top and second strands. Those of us in antelope country need to pay as much attention to the bottom of the fence as the top because, unlike deer, pronghorn are much more comfortable crawling under a fence than they are jumping over it. The bottom strand should be at least sixteen inches off the ground. While the middle wire (or wires) may be barbed, the top and bottom strands should be smooth, since these will contact passing animals, whether leaping over or shinnying beneath. If possible, the top strand should be made visible, either by using a white wire or by means of any of a variety of simple flagging techniques.

That's it. The modified fence I've just described will effectively keep cattle or horses in (or out) in most situations, and will generally be no more expensive to construct (and often less expensive to maintain) than the hazardous barricades we're currently building. If you have fencing needs not related to cattle or horses—or if you don't like the design I've suggested here—there are still many affordable ways to make your fencing safer for wildlife. These include seasonal and/or moveable electric wire fence, high-tensile electric fence, modified post and rail fence, wire suspension fence, adjustable fence, underpasses and goat bars, lay-down fence, PVC fence, dropped rail fence, and modified worm fence. The main thing to know is that a fence can accomplish whatever you need it to while also being cost-effective and wildlife friendly.

Will Rogers once observed that there are three kinds of people: "The one that learns by reading. The few who learn by observation. The rest of them have to pee on the electric fence for themselves." But when we fail to consider the effects of the kinds of fences we build, it is not we who are harmed by the fence but rather the deer and the antelope, the grouse and owls. With a little thought about how we mark and enclose our territory, we can declare our own freedom without depriving the wild things of theirs.

COWBOYS AND ALIENS

OUR YOUNGER DAUGHTER, Caroline, has a knack for inventing characters, which she animates with distinctive traits, attitudes, accents, and even signature catch phrases. Among a half dozen others there's a crotchety old lady named "Grandma Chuck," a nameless, bloviating Scotsman (complete with a thick brogue), and Guido, a pizza impresario whose Sicilian, Jersey-inflected catchphrase is "If it ain't my pie, fuggidabawdit!" Lately, though, Caroline has come up with an entirely new persona, this one a space alien who, in an irony clear enough to grown-ups, she tells us is named "Norm."

Norm is far from the norm in every way. He has a wonderful, modulating, guttural voice, as if his vocal chords were pitched to perform in a very different atmospheric pressure and gravitational field than the one here on earth. Norm can answer any question you might have about his home planet, and his replies are so amusing that Caroline's big sister, Hannah, keeps the questions coming. What does Norm like to eat? Earwax, belly button lint, and toenail clippings, though here on Earth he must occasionally resort to pinecones. What does he like best about Nevada? The ground is firm rather than spongy, as on his home planet, and is thus much better for hiking. What is his greatest frustration with living in Nevada? He hasn't managed to find a cowboy hat that will fit his enormous, bulbous alien noggin. Norm is also a bit of a rascal, often using his professed ignorance of human customs to excuse his poor table manners, failure to finish his homework, or unwillingness to make his bed. I confess that it is difficult to lay down the law when I'm laughing at the same time.

When Norm joined our family I was reminded of the most prominent alien from my own youth, the waddling, endearing little creature from Steven Spielberg's 1982 summer blockbuster *ET*. Eryn and I decided that we would screen this pop gem for the girls, just to see what Norm's reaction might be. In watching *ET* again I was reminded of the film's power to elicit our sympathy with the little alien. ET is a creature who is lost, who wants only to find his home, who feels isolated, misunderstood, uncertain, and insecure. That is to say, he's a lot like us earthlings. We empathize with ET because he feels *alienated*, a term that speaks both to his condition and to our own. Equally important, his appearance in the enchanted woods that survive along the edge of a homogenous, suburban subdivision reinforces what every kid knows instinctively: there is magic just beyond the asphalt fringes of the adult world. Hannah and Caroline loved the film, and when it reached its happy ending I asked Norm what he thought of it. "I know ET," he replied. "He visited my planet one time. His real name is Earl."

Caroline, along with Spielberg, might be forgiven for her fascination with creatures from outer space. After all, American popular culture has long been obsessed with aliens, which have provided reliable fodder for novels, movies, comics, video games, and TV shows. Occasionally we are terrified by these aliens, as in Orson Welles's infamous 1938 radio performance of H. G. Wells's *The War of the Worlds*, or the obscenely profitable Roland Emmerich flick *Independence Day* sixty years later. Sometimes we love these other-worldly beings, as in the Spielberg classic that our daughters so enjoyed. Aliens are a durable staple of our entertainment culture and also an important part of our imaginative landscape. The other day I noticed something that redoubled my certainty about the centrality of the alien in our daily lives: my smart phone has an alien-head emoji, right there next to the similarly iconic happy face. An alien emoji. Too late to turn back now, earthlings!

Here in Nevada our obsession with aliens is everywhere evident. Our state leads the nation in UFO sightings, extraterrestrial abduction conspiracy theories, and alien spacecraft recovery and cover-up narratives. Perhaps this is because we Nevadans aren't the least bit afraid of bizarre, creepy, insane stuff—as anyone who has visited the Las Vegas strip can attest. Nope, we roll out the red carpet for aliens here. We welcome them much as we do other odd tourists, high rollers visiting from out of town, looking for the kind of good time they can't get back in their home galaxy.

It is in fact a Nevada tradition to name things in honor of this most interesting of the many strange visitors we receive. Nevada State Route 375 has been officially designated "The Extraterrestrial Highway," and that lonely road goes through the little desert town of Rachel ("UFO capitol of the world"), where I'd recommend that you stop for a cold one at the Little A'Le'Inn. (After all, the hand-painted sign out front proclaims "Earthlings Are Welcome!") Our state even boasts an intergalactically themed brothel, the Alien Cathouse, located an hour north of Vegas on highway 95. Here patrons may select from any number of themed rooms, including the "Holodeck" and . . . wait for it . . . the "Alien Abduction Probing Room." If this artifact of cultural bricolage doesn't strike you as proof positive that aliens have invaded our collective fantasy life, then just try to push this one out of your mind and instead focus on cute little ET.

We Nevadans also have a legitimate reason to be cozy with this kind of fantasy, because we've had more actual UFOs in our skies than has any other state. The term *UFO*, which began to see wide use during the Cold War, simply means "unidentified flying object." Since its establishment as a top-secret military base back in 1954, Area 51 has produced about as many UFOs as has Hollywood. In response to a Freedom of Information Act filing, in 2013 the CIA for the first time acknowledged the existence of this remote, inaccessible, and heavily guarded detachment of Edwards Air Force Base. What they do not reveal, but is generally accepted, is that well before they were made public, a number of remarkable experimental aircraft—including the U2, A-12, SR-71 Blackbird, and F117-A—have been tested here. If we Nevadans have seen our share of little green men, we've also seen more than our share of unidentifiable, unimaginably futuristic military aircraft and hovercraft, the sorts of machines you would expect to see on a theater screen rather than streaking weirdly across the desert sky.

It is more than just extravagantly expensive aerial weaponry that sustains our imagination of alien visitors; it is also the landscape itself. The Great Basin Desert is so remote, isolated, and uninhabited—so open, barren, and wild—that out here anything seems possible. To a human mode of perception evolved to appreciate shelter, cover, forage, and water, this is in fact an *alien landscape*, one that we visit much as we might visit the broken, desolate surface of a distant planet. In a landscape that makes us feel like intergalactic voyagers, perhaps the idea of other strange visitations appears more plausible. Clearly, the myth of the extraterrestrial visitor is central to our cultural imagination in this part of the desert West.

Another of the most durable myths in this landscape is that of the cowboy. Perhaps some of you were unfortunate enough to have been subjected to the abysmal 2011 "science fiction western" movie *Cowboys and Aliens*. Even Harrison Ford couldn't save this bomb, which detonates stinkage for an interminable 118 minutes in the most convoluted and ludicrous plot ever to ooze from the cracks in the southern California dream factory. The movie had everything going for it: not just Ford but also Ron Howard as a producer, Spielberg as an executive producer, and a budget of 163 million dollars (maybe we should instead have used the money to build experimental aircraft?). Nevertheless, *Cowboys and Aliens* is the worst genre mash-up in cinema history, not only unsuccessfully force fitting the conventions of sci-fi and western but also gratuitously tossing in an Apache medicine man and, God help us all, a few resurrected nude corpses.

But if *Cowboys and Aliens* is an epic fail that has stolen from my mortality allowance two precious hours I'll never recover, I can't help feeling that somehow this terrible picture was on the right track. After all, both cowboys and aliens are among the most mythologized, glorified, and iconic figures in the American West. They seem to belong in this landscape, even when we aren't sure if we do. Both figures come from afar, across the wide-open spaces, and both seem dauntingly independent and self-reliant. Both depend upon their trusty steed: one an Appaloosa or Pinto, the other a whirling silver disk or darting interstellar trapezoid. Both are packing serious weapons and are defined by their ability to use them, for what is a flesh-dissolving laser if not a simple upgrade of a Walker Colt revolver? Both figures are powerful and dangerous, and yet somehow also enticingly mysterious and charismatic. They ramble from town to town, galaxy to galaxy, knocking back a little red-eye, harvesting a few human organs, just trying to get the lay of a new land. Part of their mystique is that neither sticks

HOW TO CUSS IN WESTERN

around for long, invariably galloping or whizzing off to the western horizon, or beyond it.

The main thing cowboys and aliens have in common is that both come in search of new frontiers of knowledge, experience, or power. Both represent a myth of movement, domination, and possession. The cowboy and the alien both come to the American West as colonizers. Perhaps we love the cowboy because he represents our successful colonization of this region; perhaps we fear the alien because he instead represents a terrifying desire to colonize *us*. The cowboy embodies a utopian myth of unlimited freedom, the alien a dystopian myth of inescapable captivity. Who better to fight off the invading aliens than cowboys, they who were the vanguard of the last wave of invading aliens?

I really don't mind having a daughter who is a space alien. Many Nevadans apparently believe that extraterrestrials have already hybridized with normal humans—just like the cowboys did—so perhaps that spaceship has already sailed in any case. But out here in this vast desert landscape, so bright with uncertainty, one thing is definite. I'll be taking Norm to our favorite tack and boot shop to have him custom sized for that enormous buckaroo Stetson.

TRIAL BY JURY

WHENEVER I RECEIVE a summons to jury duty, I respond to it truthfully—which is to say, I respond to it in ways that would appear, to any normal person, to be so ideological, polemical, overzealous, and doctrinal as to appear perfectly insane. But I rationalize that a functional democracy depends upon the candor of its citizens, and so, in the questionnaire sent to me by the county, I express exactly what is on my mind. Eryn suspects that my intemperate replies have prevented me from ever actually being called to join a jury, much as I have always wanted to serve. I, on the other hand, blame her family, which consists exclusively of public-interest activists and cops, all of whom intersect with the judicial system in ways that make them biased—though, in their defense, their biases cancel each other out, with one half of the family helping out the same folks whom the other half of the family tackles and cuffs.

Recently, however, I was actually *summoned to appear*, a phrase I love so dearly that I now use it to call Hannah and Caroline to breakfast. On the morning I was to *appear* I was so excited by the prospect that I even dressed properly (cowboy boots, clean denim, and an unwrinkled shirt constituting formal attire in the desert West), and I gathered a legal pad, a pen, and—just to be an especially responsible citizen—an extra pen. Over breakfast, I waxed rhapsodic to my rather bored daughters, extolling with unbridled enthusiasm the inspiring virtues of our democratic judicial system. Now, at last, I would have my own hands on the wheels and pulleys of justice, working together with my fellow citizens to produce a fair outcome for some yet unknown person whose fate would hang in the balance. As I descended Ranting Hill in my seventeen-year-old, juniper-green pickup, I hollered joyfully out the window to the girls, "The Revolution was not fought for nothing!"

My patriotic fervor was instantly dampened by the scene I encountered upon arriving at the county seat. A line of people trailed out the front door of the courthouse and wrapped around the corner, and to a person they looked as if they had been up all night drinking cheap liquor. One portly man, who was wearing rainbow-colored suspenders over a torn T-shirt, had a ring with approximately two hundred keys dangling from his belt down almost to the sidewalk. A young woman wearing work boots and Carhartt dungarees was also sporting what can only be called a tube top. Another guy had a beard so long and gray that he had to have come either from ZZ Top or 1849. An otherwise respectable-looking, middle-aged man wore a tweed jacket with elbow patches, which was fine, but on his head was a deerstalker—that weird, double-brimmed hat that is worn only by people who are costumed as Sherlock Holmes for Halloween. When a middle-aged woman, who looked like the only sane person in the lot, turned around, her hoodie sweatshirt revealed an image of Minnie Mouse, complete with polka-dotted dress, pink bow in hair, arm up, and middle finger extended. These were my fellow citizens, which made me wonder what the criminals around here might look like.

Once inside the chambers with this motley bunch, the judge and attorneys began the jury selection process, which I found fascinating. After all, it was easier to see why most of us should *not* be allowed to judge anybody than why we should. Soon enough, the dismissals began. One man knew the witnesses. Another spoke no English. A woman swore loudly that she would need to pee every fifteen minutes for the duration of the trial. A young guy said he didn't believe in government at all but wanted the forty dollars per day they would pay us to serve. Then, to the considerable exasperation of the judge, the guy wearing the deerstalker explained, in an obviously fake British accent, that he was urgently needed down at Area 51 to perform an autopsy on the remains of an alien whose wrecked spacecraft had recently been recovered by the NSA. I realized, suddenly, that I was the least weird person in the room. This was an entirely new experience for me, and I didn't like it one bit.

On this went, with folks being dismissed left and right, until the plaintiff's attorney, informing the jury that one of the witnesses was a minister, asked if anyone was so biased against religion as to find it impossible to listen objectively to a minister's testimony. At this point, approximately half of the remaining potential jurors raised their hands, prompting the judge to intervene.

"We aren't asking if you attend church, which church you attend, or even if you believe in a deity. We're asking only if you can listen without bias to the testimony of a fellow citizen who happens to be a minister. This testimony will in no way be related to religion. Please raise your hand only if you remain so biased as to be unable to perform your civic duty here today."

Now all the same hands went up, plus one more—that of a hungover-looking guy who had apparently just regained consciousness. At this point the judge, who was clearly aggravated, began a series of ambitious attempts to impress upon these recalcitrant would-be jurors the importance of their task. Did they understand that our judicial system is the envy of countries around the world, where people languish in prison simply for speaking their minds? The reply was a nodless sea of blank stares. Did they understand how rarely our citizens are asked to perform this vital civic duty and how foundational it is to the core principle of fairness upon which true justice depends? If anything, the jaws slackened a bit. At last, the judge had recourse to baseball metaphors, which indicated pretty clearly that he was running out of ideas. "Would you say that an umpire in a baseball game couldn't be trusted to call balls and strikes simply because he believes in God?"

Although the judge had not asked for it, the same group of folks raised their hands again, a little higher this time, including the recently awakened guy and now even one more lady, who was wearing an "Aces" baseball cap. The judge rocked back in his big leather chair and rubbed the temples of his lowered head between his thumb and forefingers.

"Someday, you'll be at a barbecue or a ball game," he said slowly, in a very tense voice, "and you'll hear people complain about what's wrong with our judicial system. Well, now you know. You're all dismissed!"

People think I am joking when I say that I do not like leaving Ranting Hill—that I would rather stay out here in the sticks than come to town—that, if I had my way, I might never come to town again. As a confirmed desert rat, I would rather be hungry and thirsty in a windstorm with a pack of howling coyotes than be in town for free drinks and dinner. But the dark side of this otherwise salutary isolation is that it may lead, incrementally, to the rainbow suspenders, the 1849 beard, or the deerstalker cap. I understand that we are bound by a social contract—that we have a civic duty to perform when the otherwise invisible state *summons us to appear*. But there is an odd sense in which these social relations seem abstract to those of us who live long enough in the West's remote deserts, where we forge primary allegiances to silence, weather, night sounds, alpenglow, imagination, the pungent scent of sage. We are not joiners; on the contrary, we secede religiously. I don't mean to say that Henry Thoreau was necessarily right when he concurred with the maxim "That government is best which governs least." In fact, the experience of being summoned to appear has caused me to wonder if our fierce independence may be a real threat—even to forms of social organization that ultimately protect our freedoms rather than endangering them.

I find it helpful to address this kind of question using RIs. RIs are "Rhode Islands," a unit of measurement we Great Basinians sometimes use to convey the vastness of our place in the big West. For example, at more than 110,000 square miles, Nevada comprises roughly one hundred RIs. The county in which I live, and from which my fellow jurors and I had been randomly selected, has an RI factor of six. What does it mean to live in a county six times the size of a US state? It means that you might be asked to drive hundreds of miles through a snowstorm from your remote desert home to the courthouse at the other end of this long, narrow county to perform your civic duty.

The vexing relationship between independence and interdependence can be difficult to discern. Seen in the shimmering immensity of this high desert landscape, even a town with a courthouse comes to seem like an abstraction, until—and sometimes even after—you've arrived there. Is it any wonder that some of us have gone so feral that we are now beyond the reach of baseball metaphors? Come to think of it, my fellow jurors seemed just as fascinated by my weirdness as I was by theirs. If I can at least say I have not reached the alien autopsy stage of rural desert living, it may be that I have already traveled farther down the unmarked gravel road to Area 51 than I'd like to admit.

CLOSING THE MOUNTAIN

O UT HERE IN the windy expanse of the wild Great Basin, highway 395 is our lifeline. Not simply the route south to Mono Lake and Yosemite, and north to the Lassen lava lands and Shasta country beyond, it is also the only way we can access diapers, tractor parts, beer—anything that can't be beamed to us from a satellite. Our remote home here on Ranting Hill rests within a labyrinth of ridges and canyons on the eastern flank of our home mountain, which trends north–south and carries the Nevada-California state line along its rocky crest. On this side of the mountain is a classic, high-elevation desert landscape—a sandy, expansive ocean of sagebrush dotted with bitterbrush, rabbit-brush, and ephedra, gooseberry, desert peach, and chokecherry. On the west side of the mountain is a broad, sweeping valley through which runs the distant highway, curving past the lone outpost of Hallelujah Junction. Beyond the highway to the west is the pitched escarpment of the Sierra Nevada, which rises dramatically in a heavily forested palisade of sheer granite turrets and crags.

Many world religions recognize sacred mountains, high places of spiritual power or significance. Mt. Sinai is vitally important to Judaism because it was upon this mountain that Moses is said to have received God's commandments. Likewise, Mt. Kailash to Hinduism, for that consecrated peak is considered to be the home of Shiva. The Greeks considered Mt. Olympus holy, and the Romans worshipped Mt. Etna as the abode of Vulcan, the God of fire. The Shinto of Japan pay homage to Mt. Koya-san, while the Taranaki people of New Zealand worship Mt. Taranaki, and the Nepalese deify the 23,000-foot-tall Machapuchare. Sacred mountains are also foundational to the cosmologies of many Native American peoples, including the Navajo.

Because sacred mountains are so often identified as special sites of inspiration, revelation, and transformation, many rituals have developed to honor them. Holy mountains, which are sometimes venerated as living entities, are often worshipped through practices that involve walking. For example, Buddhist and Hindu devotional practice includes the *kora*, a ritual circumambulation of sacred peaks by which the devotee makes a pilgrimage not *to* or *up* the mountain but instead *around* it. This ritual of walking meditation, which is always performed clockwise in order to follow "the way of the sun," is said to "open the mountain." One of the most famous North American circumambulations occurred in 1965, when the American poets Gary Snyder, Allen Ginsberg, and Philip Whalen made a sacramental pilgrimage around Mt. Tamalpais, on the Marin Peninsula north of San Francisco. It is a lovely ritual hike, one I have repeated many times, pausing at particular spots to read from the stanzas Gary Snyder wrote about those same spots, made sacred in his poem "The Circumambulation of Mt. Tamalpais."

Because our home mountain is twenty miles long and is surrounded by broken flanks of foothills and canyons—not to mention a few ranches where a meditating circumambulator might get a load of buckshot in his britches—rather than opening the mountain I have instead made it an annual ritual to close the mountain before the first snow renders its summit inaccessible until April or even May. Closing the mountain requires a long hike; but, as the comedian Stephen Wright has observed, "Everywhere is within walking distance if you have the time." To honor my home mountain, I hike from Ranting Hill all the way over the mountain's high crest and down to Hallelujah, a ten-mile-long transect of the range that lifts me to almost 8,000 feet before dropping down the mountain's steep western face and, eventually, all the way to the highway, which snakes through the distant valley below. Much like the bear, my annual ritual is to anticipate winter by going over the mountain just to see what I can see. Although in closing the mountain I am a transect-ambulator rather than a circumambulator, my pilgrimage, like the kora, is a devotional gesture of respect and veneration for my home mountain.

I was recently set to make the mountain-closing trek over the ridge with fellow desert rats Cheryll and Steve, when the night before the hike an early season storm descended, blanketing the desert with low clouds and bringing a hammering rain that sent water coursing through the forking network of gullies that branches through this open desert like veins. Concerned that winter might beat us to the summit, we decided to try our mountain transect despite the ominous weather.

We set out early, trudging through the driving rain, carrying oversized day packs stuffed with extra clothes and food. Three miles into the muddy slog we reached the soggy, wildfire-scorched bitterbrush flats at the base of the mountain, and from there began an 1,800-foot ascent into the chilling fog. By the time we reached the small spring halfway up the mountain we were thoroughly soaked, and had already pulled on gloves, hats, and every piece of spare clothing we had. Looking homeward across the Great Basin through the drifting fog, we caught occasional glimpses of the broken hills and sagebrush-dotted sand flats rolling east to the gray horizon. Above us to the west wound a faint game trail, rising through copses of bitter cherry and coyote willow as it skirted between slick granite cliffs that gleamed in the rain.

By midafternoon we crested the summit ridge and entered a sweeping valley that is slung gracefully between two rocky peaks and is graced with groves of gnarled aspens and surrounded by the green domes of snowberry bushes. I tried to imagine this same spot in July, when the magnificent expanse of this hanging valley would be covered in an undulating, yellow blanket of flowering tower butterweed. But now the situation was more threatening than pastoral. The valley appeared ominous as the fog lowered, the freezing rain turned to snow, and a cutting wind rose from the western flank of the mountain.

"Looks like big weather," Steve observed, squinting.

"Way too exposed," Cheryll added. "Time to skedaddle."

Shivering, I nodded my agreement. I had already begun to lose sensation in my toes, and it was obvious that we needed to head for lower country, and that without delay.

The three of us now set to hiking with intense concentration, knowing that even a short pause would be an invitation to hypothermia. We soon reached the far side of the summit valley, from which we hoped our descent of the mountain's western slope would begin. Instead, we found ourselves staring down a precipitous, brush-choked ravine that was far too thick to bushwhack. Our only alternative was to ascend a steep boulder field to a secondary ridge from which it appeared that a route down the mountain might be possible. The numbness in my feet had now overtaken my legs, and my fingers also began to deaden. It was far too late to turn back and still arrive home before dark,

HOW TO CUSS IN WESTERN

and so we began to pick our way up and over boulders slick with rime. Moving with silent urgency, I suspect we were all thinking the same thing: under these dangerous conditions, even a minor injury would quickly become a major emergency.

After another hour of climbing I was out of breath and dangerously wet and cold, but I could now make out the crest of the boulder field etching the horizon above me. At last reaching its top I clambered out onto an exposed ridge, where I noticed among the first flakes of sticking snow the scat of pronghorn antelope and that of black bear within a few feet of each other—a reminder that the keystone species of the Great Basin and Sierra Nevada overlap on this ecotonal range. If my home mountain is sacred, as it seems to me to be, that is because it is the enchanted place where the magisterial worlds of mountain and desert abide together.

Emerging onto the ridge, I first looked back across Nevada. Somewhere out among those endless, fog-shrouded ridges was a small hill, atop which sat the warm sanctuary of our home, where I pictured my beautiful daughters reading by the woodstove. And then I turned west, gazing out over rain-drenched California, spectacular in the lowering storm. Beneath the ceiling of dark clouds I now saw the ridge descend before me, narrow and sinuous as a dragon's back but clear and passable, even as steep canyons dropped precipitously away from it on either side. Beyond the serpent's curving spine lay a broad valley through which ran the gleaming asphalt trail of the highway. Only about four miles away, but nearly 3,000 feet below me, the ribbon of asphalt looked as peaceful as a miniature stream, with insect cars floating along it, and occasionally the tiny box of an eighteen-wheeler passing through the shining, black artery like a rectangular bubble. I tried to imagine the folks inside those cars and trucks. How warm they must be. How sweet must be the sound of the music pouring out of their radios. What lives they might be escaping from or returning to. Whether they turned their heads far enough to notice the desolate beauty of my home mountain rising above them into the freezing fog.

The rest of that stormy afternoon we ran the winding ridge toward the highway below, warming quickly as we dropped in elevation, descending to safety and leaving behind us a wilderness of peaks and ridges that would soon be buried beneath the season's first snow. Glancing over my shoulder occasionally as I hiked, I felt winter nipping at my heels, closing my home mountain behind me as I strode for the lowlands.

Reaching the sage flats, we bushwhacked through open desert scrub for several miles, our boots thawing out and then caking with mud. In a short time, we reached Hallelujah Junction, an isolated roadside outpost that certainly lived up to its name on that freezing afternoon. As I pushed open the swinging door of the little store I smelled warm buttered popcorn and heard men talking idly of weather, of the miles of highway behind them or that still lay ahead. The sound of a football game crackled from a small television that sat on the checkout counter between a rack of keychains and a Plexiglas container of smoked jerky.

Steve and Cheryll and I circled the small, warm space, and then stepped to the counter carrying the kinds of things Hallelujah specializes in. I bought a box of strawberry frosted pop tarts and a small bottle of whiskey, which I emptied into a large cup of ink-black coffee. Hallelujah! We have closed the consecrated mountain. Our ritual transect-ambulation has brought this season to an end, even as another has already silently begun.

Whenever I drive the Hallelujah stretch of highway, my memory triggers the aromatic smell of that bone-warming, bourbon-laced coffee. And that causes me to look up into my home mountain's towering canyons and imagine granite and lichen, bitterbrush and aspen, willow and chokecherry, pronghorn and bear. And three shivering hikers, huddled on a windy ridge in the swirling snow, looking down with relief on the gleaming, ribboned black snake of a distant highway.

PLEISTOCENE REWILDING

IN A CO-WRITTEN ARTICLE published in a major scientific journal, a small herd of perfectly respectable conservation biologists proposed a bold ecological restoration project they call "Pleistocene Rewilding." The concept itself is outrageously wild. "Rewilding" is the process of reintroducing species to ecosystems from which they have been extirpated—often by that big bully, *Homo notsosapiens*. Think of wolves being brought back to Yellowstone, or Ted Turner replacing cattle with bison on his ranches (which total 2 million acres) in the Rockies and on the Great Plains. *Pleistocene* rewilding, by contrast, is the incredible idea that we humans can enhance an ecosystem's health by reintroducing many of the large mammals that were driven to extinction between ten thousand and thirteen thousand years ago.

The so-called "pre-Columbian benchmark" of 1492 has been the commonly used target for ecosystem restoration efforts. To achieve this benchmark, scientists simply figure out how the world looked on the day that Señor Columbus made landfall—say, at about cocktail hour—and then restore North American ecosystems to that condition by extirpating exotic species, reintroducing natives, and restoring habitat. It isn't easy to do, but at least it's easy to understand. Then, along come these provocative Pleistocene Rewildatators, who ask why we are stuck on 1492 when the real trouble started thirteen millennia ago. They point out that the mass extinction of megafauna during the Pleistocene—along with a secondary wave of extinctions resulting from the disappearance of those keystone species—caused severe damage to the fabric of North American ecosystems, which some say have been slowly fraying and unraveling ever since. Since the fossil record gives us a good idea of what beasts roamed here before the arrival of human hunters from Asia (our Native Americans), why not leave Columbus out of it and select an ecological restoration benchmark that is closer to Pleistocene cocktail hour? Why not acknowledge that North American ecosystems are full of holes—ecological niches that have gone unoccupied for at least ten thousand years—and then do our best to fill those holes by reintroducing large mammals?

Now here is the fun part. It turns out that, by the time Columbus showed up, much of the cool stuff was long gone, and in this sense the usual pre-Columbian benchmark for restoration actually describes a world in which biodiversity was already radically impoverished. Pleistocene North America was home to a living bestiary of outrageous creatures, including various species of horses, donkeys, camels, muskoxen, sloths, tapirs, peccaries, cheetahs, lions, and Proboscideans (mammoths and mastodons), not to mention giant short-faced bears, ferocious saber-toothed cats, fierce dire wolves, and, to depart from mammals, the nine-foot-long sabertooth salmon and the ten-foot-tall terror bird as well. Among the charismatic megafauna that made it through the bottleneck of Pleistocene extinctions are animals we know to be equally fantastic: coyote and wolf, bison and grizzly, cougar and pronghorn antelope, to name just a few.

But these survivors are not the same without their lost neighbors. Take pronghorn, for example, a remarkable animal that can run up to sixty miles per hour. Coyotes, wolves, mountain lions, and all other predators in North America are so incredibly slow compared to pronghorn that predation by these animals simply cannot have provided the selection pressure necessary to create the pronghorn's incredible speed. Where, then, did this amazing speed come from? From the extinct American cheetah, which, although it has been absent from North American ecosystems for at least ten thousand years, chased the hell out of pronghorn for almost twenty million years before that.

Although the American cheetah and many other Pleistocene megafauna are long gone, advocates of Pleistocene Rewilding believe we can use "extant conspecifics and related taxa" (read: kinfolk) to represent extinct species in North American ecosystems. While the several species of Pleistocene tapirs are extinct, for example, they could be represented by the mountain tapir, which survives today in South America. The extinct North American camel could be replaced by the dromedary out here in the Great Basin Desert and by the vicuña or guanaco in more mountainous parts of the West.

Pleistocene North America was also home to mammoths and mastodons, megaherbivores that played an important role as keystone species. If it sounds crazy to suggest that modern elephants might be used to fill this empty ecological niche, consider this: Asian elephants are more closely related to extinct North American mammoths than they are to surviving African elephants. For the vanished American cheetah and American lion, we could simply use their African cousins. Finding big cats to reintroduce would not be difficult, since more than one thousand cheetahs are currently kept in the United States, and more lions live on private Texas ranches than in all American zoos combined.

Rewilding has already begun in North America, if we count several successfully reintroduced species. After the peregrine falcon was driven to the brink of extinction as a result of exposure to the pesticide DDT during the 1950s and '60s, populations were recovered through the introduction of seven subspecies from the United States, Europe, South America, and Australia—subspecies that served effectively as "proxy taxa" for the vanished midwestern peregrine falcon. Or consider the California condor, which was widely distributed in North America during the Pleistocene but afterward survived only along the West Coast. After successful reintroduction in California, the condor was subsequently reintroduced to the Southwest, where the species had enjoyed no prolonged residency for ten millennia.

Or, take that iconic animal of the American West, the wild mustang. Horses, which are native to North America but went extinct here twelve thousand years ago, were reintroduced by Spaniards during the late fifteenth century. The wild mustangs I sometimes see out here in Silver Hills are descendants of the conquistadores' steeds and, consequently, are generally considered non-native. But if we adjust our timescale from the pre-Columbian benchmark to the Pleistocene—if we wind the clock back from five centuries ago to 125 centuries ago—we might say that Señor Columbus and his compadres were innovators in Pleistocene Rewilding. In Nevada, we have intense controversy over BLM "gathers," roundups of non-native wild mustangs from public lands. Seen in the long view, though, the problem is not that the horses are non-native but, rather, that they decimate the range because the predators with which they coevolved have been absent for millennia. We do not have too many horses; we have too few lions.

I get it that sticking a bunch of lions and tigers and bears (Oh, my!) in Nevada might have complications. But I see no reason why legitimate scientific counterarguments should stand in the way of the imagination. What would it be like to hike Silver Hills and see not only pronghorn, as I often do, but pronghorn using every fiber of their evolutionary speed to outrun a cheetah in hot pursuit? What if a visit to our spring in the nearby foothills meant not dodging fly-encrusted cow pies but instead witnessing elephants spraying spring water on their leathery, weathered backs? What if a resident herd of camels gnawed up some of these invasive woody shrubs and restored open grasslands where cattle have left little besides thistle and cheat grass? What if it became a Fourth of July tradition to drink white Russians made with camel's milk and smoke juicy peccary sausages and tasty tapir steaks on the barbeque?

I hold no truck with the argument that we should not introduce these megafauna because they are dangerous. Already I must keep rattlers from striking my goofy dog, coyotes from attacking our lazy cat, and cougars from pouncing on the children. I think we would all be energized and invigorated by making the salutary transition from Couch Potato to Potential Prey. While I would not wish misfortune on any of my neighbors—because I have so few that I can't afford to lose too many—I would welcome the use of lions to purge Silver Hills of folks who do not do their fair share of work on our dirt road. And, maybe, the guy who talks too much down at the mailboxes. And, for sure, the lady who misdelivers the mail.

But enough rhapsodizing on the utility of lions. What I really mean to say is that to inhabit a landscape fully—especially one as remote and inhospitable as the one that is our home—requires sustained experiential contact punctuated by sudden leaps of imagination. If the Great Basin Desert impresses us with the sheer, incomprehensible vastness of its space, it is also important to triangulate this place within the vastness of time. To envision Silver Hills as it was thirteen thousand years ago is also to imagine what it might look like thirteen thousand years from now. Why only think long and hard about our place when we might also think deep about it?

I am not saying that Pleistocene Rewilding will work right away. I realize it might take ten or twelve millennia, and that a few of the neighbors—perhaps even me—will have to be sacrificed for the good of the megafauna. But think of it conceptually rather than literally. *Rewilding*: to become wild again after having lost wildness. That is a form of restoration we all need, and the first step in rewilding must be to reintroduce the possibility of the marvelous to our imagination of the land.

UNCLE HEDGIE

FOR A SOLID YEAR NOW, since last Christmas, Caroline has been pleading with us to get her a pet hedgehog. No one in the family can figure out where she got this idea in the first place. "Hedgehog" has certainly never crossed my mind, let alone my lips, but it is deep within Caroline's nature to grasp an idea and refuse to let it go. Like a weasel or gator with jaws clenched, she is incapable of giving up, a quality that makes her difficult to live with and also, in some small, important way, my hero.

As this Christmas approached, Caroline redoubled her efforts to get me to relent on the hedgehog, which meant that the hedgehog "discussion," as Eryn still insisted civilly upon calling it, had devolved into a Neanderthal battle between two of the most stubborn people ever to walk these bare, snowy hills. Tenacious little Caroline tried every angle; I was equally unyielding.

"Dad, hedgehogs are the coolest animals ever to be on Earth. Wait until you see *how* cool. It's going to blow it out your mind!"

"Honey," I replied, "we have hens that don't lay eggs, a cat that won't chase mice, and a dog that drools in gallons rather than ounces. The last thing we need is another useless pet to take care of."

"Well, Daddy, I'm not sure I care for your attitude," she observed coolly, turning one of my own pet locutions against me.

"Why can't you just want a bike, like a normal kid?" I asked.

"Because normal kids want bikes, like you said. But I'm *unique*! And a hedgehog is *unique*, so it's definitely the thing for me," she answered.

"Where did you learn the word *unique*?" I asked.

"Yeah, most kids my age don't know it. That's part of what makes me *unique*," she insisted proudly.

This standoff continued well into December, when Caroline came to us with what was billed as an important family announcement. She hated to have to go against our wishes, she explained, but she had decided it was necessary to skirt our opposition and instead ask Santa Claus to bring her the long-desired hedgehog. As evidence of her determination she displayed the letter she had written to Santa, which included the following appeal: "plese plese plese even though my mom says it is vary vary vary unlikely and my dad says did you bonk your head? PLESE PLESE PLESE get me a H E G H O G ! ! ! ! ! ! ! ! ! !" (Yes, exactly ten exclamation points.)

This was a new angle, and I was nonplussed. Eryn, who is considerably more intelligent than her husband, quickly pointed out to Caroline that Santa communicates regularly with parents, and that there is practical collaboration even in the magic that is Christmas morning.

Caroline stared back defiantly. "Santa knows my heart," she declared. And with that she spun on her heel and returned to her room, where she planted her shoulder against the side of her dresser and, like a football player driving a tackling dummy, began shoving it away to make room for the hedgehog's cage. Nothing we said made a lick of difference. This feisty little mule saw her new pet as a fait accompli, and so she remained perfectly resolute. "Santa knows my heart," she repeated firmly.

I have written that parenting, like jazz, is the art of improvisation, but it might just as well be glossed as an interminable series of Catch-22s. Eryn and I now faced a choice that felt epic. Through pure stubbornness, Caroline had placed us at a checkmate in which our "choice" was reduced to getting a hedgehog or blowing the lid on the Santa myth. How is it that parenting so often provides us only with this kind of "choice"?

Eryn remained respectful of my desire to live a long, happy, and entirely hedgehog-free life, and it pains me to confess that ultimately it was I who caved. One night, over a tumbler of sour mash, I told Eryn that I was not prepared to be remembered as the guy who murdered Santa. "I don't want the blood on my hands," I said, in a moment of profound cowardice. "Please help find us a damned hedgehog." And with that I poured another drink.

Arrangements were made, money changed hands, and, on the morning of December 25, there was, beneath the tree, that most precious of Christmas miracles: an unwanted pet. When Caroline raced out to the living room to see that, indeed, Santa knew her heart, the look on her face conveyed a sublime combination of pure joy and "I told you so," which, I suspect, is the only way pure joy can be improved upon.

Having learned just enough about the captive-bred hedgehog to suspect it would make a terrible pet, especially for a kid, I tried to lower Caroline's expectations without dampening her enthusiasm. "CC, I'm really happy for you. But you need to know that this isn't a warm and fuzzy pet, like a bunny. This guy is spiny, reclusive, and nocturnal. He might be hard to love."

Eryn looked at me and smiled. "Well, Bubba," she said, "there's somebody else in this family who is spiny, reclusive, and nocturnal."

"That's right," Hannah chimed in, "and we still love *you*."

I soon found myself not only reconciled to "Uncle Hedgie," as Caroline had named the little beast (though it might have been Aunt Hedgie, for all I knew), but fascinated by him. There was no denying that the thing was, to use a word I've tried in vain to scrub from my personal lexicon, *cute*. He was a spiny, little ball—larger than a baseball but smaller than a softball—with handsome salt-and-pepper coloration on his long spines. His tiny ears were delicately cupped and jet black, and his small eyes, glossy and bulbous, were also deep black. His face consisted of a long, narrow snout, which, although not very porcine, had given rise to the "hog" part of his name. The tip of the snout was polished black, with small nostrils, and graced with long, downward-curving whiskers. Hedgie's nose twitched constantly, suggesting an intelligent suspicion of the lumbering apes that gawked at him.

Most fascinating was the little beast's remarkable running ability. I had read that hedgehogs will climb onto a play wheel at night and run for hours, and that it is common for them to cover an incredible six or seven miles in a single night. This seemed unlikely for an animal with legs about the length of toothpicks, but Uncle Hedgie turned out to be a champion ultramarathoner. Each night, shortly after Caroline fell asleep, he would scamper out from hiding and jump onto his large wheel, on which he ran so hard and so long that I could often hear him racing away without pause until just after dawn.

I also admired Uncle Hedgie's bad attitude. He spent most of the day hiding under a piece of cloth, he did not enjoy being handled, and he never hesitated to prick up his spines when he was grouchy, which was most of the time. In a world full of pets bred to be affectionate and loyal—a saccharine world of kittens and puppies—here, at last, was an honest misanthrope. His best trick, which he performed at the slightest irritation, was to hiss loudly and convulse forward into a perfect ball of spines—one in which it was impossible to locate his face or his ass, or even to know whether he was in possession of either. This ability to become utterly spherical is why, in Lewis Carroll's *Alice in Wonderland*, the White Queen commits the indignity of using hedgehogs as croquet balls. Back on this side of the looking glass, I can only imagine that a predator, upon seeing this prickly ball of trouble, might just cock its head and walk away. I envied Uncle Hedgie this unassailable form of self-protection, and found myself wishing I had the capacity to deploy it during meetings at work.

The Ancient Greek poet Archilochus observed, "The fox has many tricks, and the hedgehog only one, but that is the best of all." But Archilochus obviously lived in a time before toilet paper, because our hedgehog had a second trick, and it was his best. Uncle Hedgie loved to stick his snout into a cardboard toilet paper core (which I slit with my pocket knife to prevent it from becoming permanently lodged on his noggin), after which he staggered around waving it in the air like a tiny, spiny drunk. How could I not like this little guy?

I did not confess to the family that I had been secretly nerding it up by researching hedgehogs. It turns out there are no living species native to the Americas, which is why we Yanks celebrate Groundhog Day in place of Hedgehog Day, a holiday that in Europe has inspired saturnalian revelry since the time of the Romans. What intrigued me most was the ancient pedigree of the species. Despite his weird appearance and even weirder behavior, this animal has not changed much in the past fifteen million years. Given my own notably idiosyncratic behaviors, I was filled with hope by the idea that weird had been working so well for so long. Hedgie wasn't as ancient as a sponge or a jellyfish, but fifteen million is a lot of evolutionary birthdays for a mammal. Compare this to local desert critters like coyotes and bobcats, which are a few million years old at best.

In fact, the hedgehog is so old that his resemblance to the por-cupine and echidna is simply the product of convergent evolution, which is a fancy way of saying that, because this is a harsh world in which we might all do well to be covered with protective spines, different species arrived at this physiological defense mechanism through completely unrelated evolutionary paths. Uncle Hedgie is a mammal, just like you and me—only he has been around forty or fifty times longer than we have. I could not help but respect how antediluvian this little guy was, and I came to feel that having Uncle Hedgie living with us on Ranting Hill was the equivalent of sharing our bathtub with a sturgeon or coelacanth.

If Santa knew Caroline's heart, she knew her mind. She honestly wanted nothing more for Christmas, and, having received Uncle Hedgie, she was entirely thrilled. Unlike most grown-ups, Caroline always knows what she wants in life; also unlike us, she is satisfied when she gets it. She loves to play with her *unique* pet—at least, such play as is possible with a cranky, nocturnal pincushion—and she takes good care of him. For my part, I like the way having a hedgehog forces me to remember how ridiculously young we hu-mans are as a species, and how few of our current, mostly infantile, behaviors are likely to be sustainable for the next fifteen hundred years, let alone fifteen million.

When Uncle Hedgie looks me in the eye, I detect in his glare an unmistakable message: "Back off, sonny. I've been doing my thing since you were in evolutionary short pants." If, in the impos-sibly distant future, humans are still around—and can do things like convulse into a perfect sphere of spines—then we will have earned the right to cop an attitude of superiority. In the mean-time, Uncle Hedgie has earned not only Caroline's affection but my respect.

UPON THE BURNING
OF OUR HOUSE

WHEN I SAY THAT American writers have ignited fires, I do not mean only that they have fired our imaginations or that they have sparked changes in the way we understand the world. I also mean that many of my favorite American authors actually burned stuff down. Not on purpose, of course.

In her poem "Verses Upon the Burning of Our House," the Puritan poet Anne Bradstreet described the harrowing experience she had in July 1666, when she awoke to discover her home ablaze.

> I wakened was with thund'ring noise
> And piteous shrieks of dreadful voice.
> That fearful sound of "Fire!" and "Fire!"
> Let no man know is my desire.

The power of Bradstreet's poem is in its inquiry into if and how her stuff—the material possessions destroyed by the fire—should be valued. She knows that her love of God must triumph over her love of the things of this world, and yet the poem is rich with genuine regret, because although she is relieved not to have lost her life or her faith, she also knows that material things often tether us to who we are and to those we love. Even as she resolves herself to God's will, we can feel the pain of her loss of those things to which her fondest memories are attached:

> Here stood that trunk, and there that chest,
> There lay that store I counted best.
> My pleasant things in ashes lie,
> And them behold no more shall I.

A century later, in February 1770, Thomas Jefferson's home at Shadwell, Virginia, burned in a house fire that resulted, lamented Mr. Jefferson, in the loss of "every paper I had in the world, and almost every book." When Jefferson returned to the smoldering ashes of what had been his home, his first question was, "Have my books been saved?" I can only imagine what went through the mind of eighteenth-century America's greatest bibliophile upon being informed that his library had been lost in the blaze but that a fiddle had been saved. "A fiddle?" he must have thought, "Are you fucking kidding me?" This fire may have been for the best in the long run, since Jefferson later moved up the hill from Shadwell and built a decent little place he called Monticello. I lived in Shadwell for a few years back in the mid-1980s, before I came both to the high desert and to my senses (which, for me, amounted to the same thing). Each day I would drive past Jefferson's famous neoclassical mansion on my way to my own place, which was a wood-heated, green-board shack slung low in a soggy, shadowed, hickory-choked and poison ivy–filled hollow. My digs contained an ancient woodstove, a foot-pumped bellows organ, and a giant, pulleyed candelabra, but no toilet—though I did have a borrowed goat named Melville who cropped the stinging nettle that grew along the path to the outhouse.

A century after Jefferson's Shadwell fire, the misadventure of a truly incendiary American literary figure occurred in the woods near Concord, Massachusetts, the hotbed of American Transcendentalism. In April 1844, Henry David Thoreau made a campfire on the banks of Fair Haven Bay. As usual, he had been hiking and fishing while his neighbors were living those pitiable lives of quiet desperation back in town, and now he wanted to fry his catch. Instead, he accidentally fried the neighboring woods, burning more than 300 acres of forest, threatening the town with destruction, and contributing to his already bad reputation as an irresponsible ne'er-do-well. It did not help that Thoreau remained unremorseful, later writing in his journal, "I once set fire to the woods. . . . It was a glorious spectacle and I was the only one there to enjoy it." As with Bradstreet, who turned her fire into a moving poem, and Jefferson, who turned his Shadwell loss into the architectural monument that is Monticello, art was also born of Henry's conflagration. In the wake of the fire, his neighbors so often ragged on him for his near-criminal negligence that he decided to take shelter at a nearby pond, where he had the transformative experience that produced *Walden* (1854). In this sense, fire may have indirectly inspired the creation of what is among the most influential and provocative of nineteenth-century American books.

Much closer to Ranting Hill was the wildfire accidentally ignited by Mark Twain during his visit to Lake Tahoe in the late summer of 1861. In *Roughing It*, the 1872 book in which he relates his adventures in Nevada, Twain explains that his lakeshore campfire escaped to the forest floor, where it touched off the pine needles that carpeted the ground before spreading quickly into the manzanita chaparral and raging out of control. "Within half

HOW TO CUSS IN WESTERN

an hour all before us was a tossing, blinding tempest of flame! It went surging up adjacent ridges—surmounted them and disappeared into the canyons beyond," wrote Twain. "[A]s far as the eye could reach the lofty mountain-fronts were webbed as it were with a tangled net-work of red lava streams. Away across the water the crags and domes were lit with a ruddy glare," he continues, "and the firmament above was a reflected hell!" Even though Twain was personally responsible for this hellish conflagration, he follows Thoreau in admiring the beauty produced by his carelessness. "Every feature of the spectacle was repeated in the glowing mirror of the lake! Both pictures were sublime, both were beautiful," he writes admiringly, "but that in the lake had a bewildering richness about it that enchanted the eye and held it with the stronger fascination." And, with that perceptive aesthetic appreciation, Twain joined the ranks of American literary firebugs.

Then there's my cantankerous fellow desert rat, Edward Abbey. In the hilarious, heartbreaking chapter of *Desert Solitaire* called "Down the River," Cactus Ed tells the story of his two-week raft trip through Glen Canyon in June 1959, shortly before the Colorado River was dammed to create Lake Powell. Soon after passing the mouth of the San Juan River, Abbey accidentally started a brushfire in a side canyon. He combines excitement with his signature droll humor, writing that his river buddy Ralph is "all ready to cast off, when I appear, about ten feet in front of the onrushing sheet of fire, running. I push the boats off and roll in; we paddle as hard as we can away from the fiery shore. . . . 'Hot in there,' I say, though Ralph has asked no questions." Art also rose from the ashes of Abbey's fire. As he notes in *Desert Solitaire*, "you can see a photograph of what I did in Eliot Porter's beautiful book on Glen Canyon, *The Place That No One Knew*." Canyon blazes notwithstanding, Abbey's literary art and Porter's visual art have given us a visceral understanding of what was lost when Lake Powell inundated one of the most magnificent canyon systems in the American West.

Finally, I'm reminded of the devastating 1991 Oakland Hills fire—a literal "firestorm" (a blaze so intense that it ultimately produces its own wind) that was driven by hot, dry, northeasterly Diablo winds that blasted the Oakland and Berkeley hills at more than seventy miles per hour. This fast-moving fire killed twenty-five people and destroyed more than 3,000 houses and apartment buildings. Among those who lost their home in this wildland-urban interface conflagration was the gifted Chinese-American novelist Maxine Hong Kingston, who writes beautifully about her loss in *The Fifth Book of Peace*. Kingston shares the painful story of returning through burned-over neighborhoods to the site of her home in search of the only manuscript copy (and backup disk) of a book that she had been working on for several years. Among the incinerated remnants of her home she at last discovers the remains of her book manuscript: "I touched the lines, and they smeared into powder," she recalls. "I placed my palm on this ghost of my book, and my hand sank through it. Feathers floated into the air, became air, airy nothing." Standing amid the ashes of her home and possessions, Kingston at last confronts the fatal loss of her cherished work: "My Book of Peace is gone."

We have more than our fair share of wildfires out here in Silver Hills, blazes that are usually attributable to bad mufflers, illegal off-roaders, or drunken plinkers—or, in one notorious case, the bad muffler on the illegal off-road vehicle of a drunken plinker. During the past decade, I've done countless hours of fuels reduction work on our property, removing more than a hundred dump trailer loads of sage, rabbitbrush, and juniper snags. I have maintained my firebreaks with vigilance, and I even installed perimeter hose bibs in anticipation of someday having to fight a brushfire.

But, this past Valentine's Day Eve, I was reminded that the threat of fire exists within our home, as well as out on the wildlands interface. On the evening of February 13 (Ash Wednesday, ironically enough), I joined the ranks of famous American writers when my house caught fire, which at least proves that I am willing to do whatever it takes to break into the literary pantheon.

Eryn and I had just put Hannah and Caroline to bed when the smoke alarm went off, which I assumed was nothing more than a battery issue. But when a second alarm went off upstairs, I ran up to have a look. Although I smelled no smoke, I discovered a helpful indication that there might be a problem when I observed flames shooting several feet out of the floor adjacent to the sheetrock chase containing the woodstove's chimney stack. I yelled downstairs to Eryn to call 911, wake the girls, and evacuate Ranting Hill immediately. While she was doing that, I emptied both nearby fire extinguishers into the ever-expanding hole burning through the floor, but to disturbingly little effect. I then sprinted down to the kitchen and garage and grabbed the other three extinguishers in the house, dashed back upstairs, and blasted all three of those into the flaming floor. Having exhausted my store of extinguishers, I now began a wild shuttle run from the bathtub to the fire, where I dashed five-gallon buckets of water onto the glowing floor and wall in an attempt to contain a fire that was spreading quickly. I also opened the hatch of the woodstove downstairs and tossed full buckets of water onto the hissing coals, causing choking clouds of sulfurous smoke to billow out into the house, where smoke alarms now blared from every room.

Back upstairs, thick smoke began to fill the house, even as I continued to splash water not only on the floor and wall but now also on the nearby stacks of books and papers that represented all my ongoing writing projects. After twenty-five minutes of this frantic, solo firefighting, I saw through the smoke the distant, flashing red lights of emergency vehicles making their way up the long, muddy driveway to our home.

When the firefighters arrived, they quickly suited up, oxygen tanks and all, and relegated me to the sidelines. For the next three hours I stood out in the cold, shivering as I watched a small army of masked men running in and out of our house carrying axes, hoses, and chainsaws. Smoke billowed from beneath the eaves of the roof, and I could hear chainsaws ripping into the floors, walls, and ceilings, as emergency responders chased the fire through our home. Through the windows shone headlamp beams tunneling into the smoke, but I could not see enough to know what was going on, and for a good part of the night the fate of our home remained uncertain.

Our house was ultimately saved, but not before the computers were fried, books and papers water damaged, and most of the furniture, carpets, curtains, and clothes ruined by smoke. Still, my family was safe, and our home was still standing on Ranting Hill. Even our dog and cat had survived the fire by fleeing into the open desert. It was obvious enough that it could have been much worse. What if we had not been home, or the smoke alarm had failed to work, or I didn't have on hand five fire extinguishers to slow the blaze? What if snow or mud had kept firefighters from reaching Ranting Hill? What if the bearing-wall posts supporting the roof had burned through while I fought the fire with nothing more than a bucket?

Two centuries after Thoreau's birth, no environmental writer can get completely clear of his shadow, however hard we might try. Among the most enduring elements of cranky Uncle Henry's legacy is his tireless interrogation of the value of experience as compared with the value of things. The opening chapter of *Walden*, "Economy," is as eloquent an attack on consumerism and materialism as American literature has ever produced, and any honest reader of that text is forced to examine why they own so much stuff, how much of it they actually need, and whether they might be better off if they could somehow recover the time they spent working the job to earn the money to buy the stuff, which they felt they needed to console themselves for the stress and fatigue caused by the job, which they had to keep working so they could buy the stuff.

"The cost of a thing," wrote Thoreau in *Walden*, "is the amount of what I will call life which is required to be exchanged for it, immediately or in the long run." What if we made decisions about purchases not using a definition of cost that equates stuff with dollars but, instead, by invoking this alternative definition of cost as the precious time we must sacrifice—the sheer, exquisite, irreplaceable life experiences we must forgo—in order to afford the purchase? "Shall we always study to obtain more of these things," asked Thoreau, "and not sometimes to be content with less?"

I first read *Walden* several lifetimes ago, when I was a poor graduate student at Mr. Jefferson's university, living in that Appalachian shotgun shack back in Shadwell, Virginia. The room in which I slept contained only a sleeping bag on the floor, an inverted peach crate for a side table, and a small reading lamp atop the crate. It was as austere an existence as anyone who isn't homeless or backpacking is likely to experience. And yet, so incisive was Thoreau's critique of the burden of possessions that I remember returning to my room late one night after studying *Walden*, looking down at that mummy bag and peach crate and lamp, and thinking to myself: *I don't need that damned crate.*

Now, here I was, decades later, the day after our house fire, watching load after load of damaged stuff being hauled out of our home. As the demolition and salvage work proceeded apace, it was a surreal experience to watch strangers carry charred I-beams, chainsawed wallboard, stripped carpet, and fried electronics outside, where—along with many of my books and papers—they were unceremoniously dumped in a pile in the mud in preparation for the haul out.

It was precisely because the total cost of his little home at Walden Pond was a mere $28.12½ (at a time when the average cost of a house in town was around eight hundred bucks) that Thoreau considered himself the richest man in Concord. "If my house had been burned," he observed, "I should have been nearly as well off as before." In other words, the less stuff you have, the less you have to lose, and fewer are the hours lost in fueling the acquisitive fire that consumes so much of our lives.

Like Anne Bradstreet, I care a great deal about my family's things, and I will wager that I value my books as much as Jefferson did his. I hope that, like Mark Twain and Ed Abbey, no sudden blaze can deprive me of my sense of humor, without which life's difficulties would sometimes be unbearable. And I aspire to the wisdom that graces Maxine Hong Kingston's account of the total loss of her home and her magnificent Book of Peace. But, finally, it is the voluntary simplicity of Henry Thoreau that has served me best during this trial. While I suspect I will never acquire what Thoreau considered his "greatest skill," which was "to want but little," his insistence that cost be reckoned by the standard of life itself provides a liberating insight of immense value. We have nature, which is our widest home, and those we love, and the fleeting privilege to experience both. In the end, everything else is just stuff.

RUNNING INTO WINTER

WHEN MY FATHER-IN-LAW'S sixtieth rolled around, we gathered as a family and asked what he wanted for his birthday. Without hesitating he replied, "I want you all to run a half marathon with me." I responded to this proposal as would any supportive person who cares deeply about honoring a close relation's important birthday wish: "No, seriously, what do you *really* want?"

Assured of the unhappy news that he was serious, I pointed out that the farthest I have run since age sixteen is from my writing desk to my beer fridge. Indeed, the fact that I have a beer fridge in my scribble den may help you to gauge my level of interest in long-distance running. I also observed that, from an evolutionary point of view, running only makes sense if one is chasing or being chased. He responded that since I was certain to do very poorly I would have the opportunity to chase all 6,999 of the other participants. My motivation would thus be to avoid coming in last. This did seem a compelling incentive, but still I resisted, this time telling my father-in-law that while he is a full-blooded California Central Valley Okie, running is rather a yuppie activity—unless one is running to nab a possum for the stewpot. Unpersuaded, he swiftly concluded the conversation by genially dismissing my arguments as "the sophistry of the chickenshitted."

Unfortunately for my wife and daughters, I have matured very little since age sixteen, when I dove off a ninety-foot cliff only because another kid made chicken sounds at me. So if I told you that the joke about the redneck whose last words are "Hey, y'all, watch this!" was written about me, you'd guess correctly that despite my lack of experience, interest, motivation, or fitness, I ran the hell out of that half marathon. And while three or four thousand people did cross the finish line before me, including a bunch of girl scouts, an eighty-six-year-old woman, a really friendly army vet in a wheelchair, and, of course, my father-in-law, I eventually crossed too. I was soon surfing a fat endorphin buzz, drinking free beer, and reveling in the fact that I was demonstrably not a chicken—and it wasn't even 10:00 A.M. yet. In that moment I experienced a disconcerting realization: I actually liked running.

Why disconcerting? Our home landscape in the high-elevation foothills of the western Great Basin Desert is extreme and unforgiving. It is a hard place simply to live, never mind run. Summers are hot and dusty, spring and fall can happen in the time it takes to fetch a whiskey, and the wind howls all year around. But it is winter that makes running here nearly inconceivable. I've seen it snow every month of the year except August, and it is not uncommon to have some snow on the ground from November through April. Before my half marathon euphoria even subsided, I had already begun to wonder if in becoming a runner I had started something the high desert would never let me finish.

As the snows of winter buried my hopes for running, I began to despair. The temperature of my cabin fever ran higher than usual, and even snowshoeing didn't do much for my morale. Finally, in a despondent fit I recalled a Danish maxim that had once been shared with me by the Norwegian wife of a Swedish friend while I was visiting Finland: "Det er ingenting som daarligt vejr, det er kun daarlige paaklaedning." While these words of wisdom appear on the page as if they might translate as "Those who ingest some dark beer, must eat their hairiest goat," it apparently means, "There's no such thing as bad weather, just being badly dressed for it." Perhaps I was simply ill-equipped! Certainly, there must be runners in other parts of the world who had conquered the challenge I now faced. I had a Great Basin problem, but I needed a Nordic solution.

Research led me to the Icebug, a running shoe developed in Sweden by Peter Öberg and Erik Öhlund, guys whose impressive athleticism, self-described "freakish interest in shoes," and names with umlauts were precisely the credentials I sought. The running shoe the umlaut brothers invented is fabricated from a special kind of super-grippy rubber, and includes this medieval feature: its sole is embedded with two dozen steel studs. The real trick is that these studs are not fixed in the sole but instead are pushed outward by the runner's weight as their foot flexes against a slippery surface, like twenty retracted stilettos that suddenly shoot into action when you need them most. The ad copy suggesting that I'd soon be streaking across bare ice seemed overly sanguine, but I was desperate, and so I placed my order and waited for the experiment to arrive.

My first midwinter run up into the Silver Hills was among the most memorable of my life. I dressed for the occasion, laced up the black, spiked Icebugs—which more closely resembled torture devices than running shoes—and headed out hopefully into the snow. My route would be up the BLM canyon road into the white hills above, my destination a perennial spring in a frozen valley at

about 7,000 feet. I had read that the shoes worked best on compacted snow or ice, and I knew that my misanthropic neighbor,
Ludde, had already been up the canyon road on his chained-up
ORV, breaking trail to give his ten bird dogs a slot in which to
run. And so I took off, laboring uphill through the snowbanks,
following the track made by Ludde and his pack of pointers. The
farther I ran, the better I felt, my growing elation inspired by the
feeling that the tools on my feet had opened my high home hills
in an entirely new way. The glistening gates of winter swung open
before me, and I experienced a satisfying sense that snow would
never hold me prisoner again.

Having run the three miles up to the spring, I paused there to
drink and to admire my looming home mountain, whose massive, snow-corniced brow was etched against the cobalt western
sky. The tips of bitterbrush, ephedra, and sage protruded from
the drifts here and there. A pair of glossy ravens appeared on cue,
slicing black over palisades of marbled granite on a nearby ridgeline. Then I tightened the laces on the black Icebuggies and began running down the mountain. The farther I ran, the more I
trusted the crazy shoes, and with that trust came comfort, and
with comfort speed, and with speed the return of that species of
exhilaration that is unique to running. I was alone in the expansive silence of the high desert hills, and I was streaking downhill
on naked ice, dropping toward home through a sinuous slot in an
unbroken wilderness of snow. It was my apotheosis as a runner. I
felt effortlessly strong, agile, and swift—exactly like a pronghorn,
I thought to myself. In reality I was graceless, panting, and hoof-
ing about fifty-four miles per hour more slowly than a pronghorn,
but somehow I didn't notice that at the time.

Ten years later, I still run that half marathon with my family
every fall, and I continue each year to be beaten badly by children,
and by the aged and infirm, not to mention the sound drubbing I

routinely receive from my father-in-law. But among the pleasures of running is that, when conditions are right, it is possible to enter a state of mind in which one's shortcomings cease to be relevant to the enterprise. When I lace up my Icebugs and head up into these snowy canyons, I feel unaccountably fleet and swift. As a runner I am every bit as slow and awkward as I ever was, but no matter. In those brief and shining moments, drunk on endorphins and snowy desert light, my studded soles and winged heels transform me into the Mercury of Silver Hills.

MISSIVES FROM THE HILL

THE HILL FROM WHICH I have been ranting so passionately for so many years is good for many things: to hold our house up high into the teeth of the desert wind and generate an updraft on which harriers kite; to give us the pitch necessary for quality tobogganing, and to ensure that we are snowed in often enough to enjoy it; to keep us above winter inversions so we may gaze down upon an archipelago of broken peaks emerging magically from a valley-wide, flat-topped ocean of pogonip below. Perhaps the most satisfying thing about living atop a high hill, though, is that it offers so convenient and pleasing a place to throw things off of.

Maybe I should be ashamed of my enthusiasm for heaving things off our home hilltop. But judge not, lest you be judged. How often do you feel an urge to fling something? Perhaps I am more of a hothead than the average person, but approximately every seventh time I pick up an object—a jammed stapler, ringing cell phone, cold cup of coffee, poorly written newspaper, or any of an infinite number of things that are, essentially, cheap plastic crap—I have a secret desire to launch it. Most of us have learned to repress this basic human desire to throw things, or at least to sublimate our desire into the congenial tossing of Frisbees or softballs. But I believe that we each harbor a deep longing to convert the latent energy of our daily frustrations into the more satisfying kinetic energy of a flying object. For me, the most rewarding means by which to make objects fly is to perch atop Ranting Hill and, in inspired bursts of rage, throw them as far as I can into the open desert below.

When I sing the praises of my home hill as an excellent place from which to throw stuff, I mean to advocate the chucking of objects not as mere petulance but rather as a deeply ennobling form of self-expression. Consider the etymology of the word *missile*, which, when used as an adjective, denotes an object that is "capable of being thrown"—a quality shared by nearly everything I can get my hands on when I am sufficiently irate. That word's older cousin, *missive*, derives from the Middle Latin *missivus* and was often used in the beautiful phrase *littera missiva*, which means "letters sent." When in a fine fit I heave things off my hill, I am expressing the zeal of a *missionary* (another related word) who wishes, earnestly, to send a message forth. Like these essays, which are small missives launched toward you from the crest of a remote, unnamed foothill in the western Great Basin Desert, the things I pitch off this place are dispatches. To paraphrase fellow recluse writer Emily Dickinson, they are my heartfelt letters to the world.

Most of the objects I have thrown off our hill are not letters in the conventional sense. Rather, they are missives in the form of cheap tools, broken toys, dull saw files, ugly patio furniture, dead rodents, blown-out work boots, empty ballpoint pens, nicked Kevlar chaps, or anything else that annoys me and thus seems suddenly in need of aerial relocation to packrat country in the sagebrush down below. For me, these missile launches are a survival mechanism. If I am a loving husband, patient father, devoted son, helpful neighbor, and good-humored writer, as I hope I am, that is simply because I can purge my frustrations with a healthy toss now and then. The therapeutic value of this tossing, however, depends upon the strictest solitude, which is a luxury those who live in town can scarcely afford. Like urinating outside one's home—a gesture that is a sublimely satisfying expression of personal freedom and a means by which, like writing, I mark my territory—it requires both privacy and space to hurl stuff properly. If you toss objects out of your apartment window, you are arrested; if you fling junk around your suburban yard, you are socially outcast. But here, in the open country of the desert West, you can throw whatever you can afford to do without for a while, just so long as your children aren't around to learn from your poor example.

For many years I steadfastly maintained the self-discipline to throw things off our hill only in moments of solitude, until one recent winter night when my fury overcame what shred of good sense I still possess. My mother-in-law happened to be visiting at the time, when a smoke alarm that had been giving me a world of trouble went off in the middle of the night. Bear in mind that this malfunctioning alarm had awakened my family three nights in a row, that my repeated attempts to fix it had failed miserably, that I had managed that day to get both my truck and tractor stuck in the same icy ditch, and that I had not discovered, until noon, that I had accidentally been drinking decaf all morning. When, at 2:00 A.M., this smoke alarm—which now had the formerly snoozing mother-in-law beneath it—went blaring off again, I rose slowly from my bed, walked calmly up the stairs toward the deafening chirping, stepped up onto the mother-in-law's bed (with her still in it), reached up, and with a brisk yank pulled the malfunctioning unit, wires and all, clean out of the ceiling—leaving a ragged hole from which gypsum dust rained slowly down onto my wife's mother.

HOW TO CUSS IN WESTERN

There followed a nourishing silence, during which I turned to head back to bed. In the next moment, however, the worst happened: the alarm released one final, shorted-out little beep. It was only a death chirp, really, but by this point my patience and I were both exhausted, and my decisions were being made in the part of my brain that evolved long before smoke alarms were invented. I excused myself politely from the room, calmly opened the slider door, stepped out onto the balcony, and then pretended emphatically to wipe my ass with the alarm—a dramatic gesture I need hardly add was purely instinctual—after which I heaved the device as far as I could out into the desert night. I watched with satisfaction as it sliced away into the moonlight, as if in slow motion, toward a distant juniper. Although I injured my triceps slightly on the throw, it was a moment so deeply gratifying that I find it impossible now to express fully the pleasure it brought.

Early that morning, nearly a foot of beautiful, fresh snow fell, burying the smoke alarm, along with all the other missives I had recently air-mailed into the wild desert. We won't see a melt-out for months now, but when spring finally comes—which, at this elevation, happens mighty late—Hannah and Caroline will join me on a "treasure hunt" out in the sage. What we discover there will be artifacts from a time already long past, when barely remembered moments of frustration gave wings to earthbound objects like smoke detectors and alarm clocks. We field archaeologists of Ranting Hill do not know precisely what we will discover down there, but we are already looking forward to the adventure of finding out. For now, the snow just keeps falling, and we and the earth are the better for it.

CREDITS

The "Rants from the Hill" essay series that eventually led to this book appeared in *High Country News*, where the Rants ran online every month from July 2010 through April 2016. "Shit Happens" and "My First Rodeo" were not originally included in the series and have not been published elsewhere.

Several essays were reprinted in other venues, as follows:

"Few and Far Between" contains passages from an essay originally entitled "The Silence of Desert Greetings" (May 2012). My podcast of this essay was excerpted and integrated into the *Van Sounds* podcast, edited by Fil Corbitt, episode "Dice 5: Nothing on the Radio" (January 7, 2016): http://filcorbitt.com/van-sounds.

"Walking to California." *Whole Terrain: Reflective Environmental Practice* 18 (2011): 5–7.

"Them! and Us" appeared in "Excerpts from 'Rants from the Hill.'" *The Nevada Review* 5.1 (Spring 2013): 24–28.

"Scout's Honor." *Whole Terrain: Reflective Environmental Practice* 22 (2016): 23–27.

"What Would Edward Abbey Do?" *High Country News* 43.7 (May 2, 2011): 23. Reprinted in *Utne Reader* online (June 21, 2011) and *Denver Huffington Post* online (October 2011).

"Reckoning the Ghost of Cactus Ed: Reflections on the Unforeseen Hazards of Trundling." *Whole Terrain: Reflective Environmental Practice* 20 (2013): 53–57. (Contains passages from "What Would Edward Abbey Do?")

"Executive Order: Rewilding." Island Press *Field Notes* (February 2014). http://ipfieldnotes.org/executive-orders-for-2014-michael -branch. (Contains passages from "Pleistocene Rewilding.")

"In Defense of Missiles" (here retitled "Missives from the Hill") appeared in "Excerpts from 'Rants from the Hill.'" *The Nevada Review* 4.3 (Fall 2012): 83–96.

ACKNOWLEDGMENTS

WRITERS ARE VERY MUCH IN NEED of friends, and I have been fortunate to have so many in my life and in my corner. Here I offer my sincere thanks, along with equally sincere apologies to anyone I may have neglected to include.

Among fellow writers of environmental creative nonfiction, my thanks go to Rick Bass, Paul Bogard, Taylor Brorby, John Calderazzo, SueEllen Campbell, Craig Childs, Laird Christensen, Casey Clabough, Jennifer Cognard-Black, Chris Cokinos, Alison Deming, John Elder, Tom Fate, Andy Furman, Dimitri Keriotis, Ian Marshall, Kate Miles, Kathy Moore, John Murray, Nick Neely, Sean O'Grady, Tim Palmer, Bob Pyle, David Quammen, Eve Quesnel, Brad Rassler, Janisse Ray, Suzanne Roberts, Chris Robertson, Leslie Ryan, Terre Ryan, Gary Snyder, John Tallmadge, David Taylor, Leath Tonino, Nick Triolo, and Rick Van Noy. Very special thanks to John Price, John Lane, and David Gessner, whose support has been decisive.

Thanks also for the encouragement I've received from other friends in the environmental literature and humor studies communities, including Tom Bailey, Patrick Barron, Jim Bishop, Chip Blake, Kate Chandler, Ben Click, Tammy Cloutier, Nancy Cook, Ann Fisher-Wirth, Jeanie French, Charles Goodrich, Tom Hallock, Tom Hillard, Heather Houser, Richard Hunt, Jamie Iredell, Dave Johnson, Rochelle Johnson, Talley Kayser, Peter Kopp, Jason Leppig, Nancy Levinson, Mark Long, Tom Lynch, Kyhl Lyndgaard, Annie Merrill, Clint Mohs, David Morris, Tara Penry, Dan

Philippon, Anna Lena Phillips, Justin Race, Steve Railton, Kate Rigby, Rowland Russell, Jennifer Sahn, Heidi Scott, Robert Sickels, Dave Stentiford, David Taylor, Jim Warren, Alan Weltzein, Tracy Wuster, and Boyd Zenner.

Closer to home, I'd like to offer thanks to fellow Great Basin writers Bill Fox, Shaun Griffin, Dave Lee, Mark Maynard, Ann Ronald, Rebecca Solnit, John Trent, Steve Trimble, Claire Watkins, Terry Tempest Williams, and Lindsay Wilson, with a nod to the desert writers who led my way: Mary Austin, Ed Abbey, Ellen Meloy, and Chuck Bowden. I'd also like to acknowledge the Ellen Meloy Desert Writers Fund and the Nevada Writers Hall of Fame for recognizing and helping to support my work. Thanks to my colleagues in the MFA program at the University of Nevada, Reno: David Durham, Steve Gehrke, Sarah Hulse, Ann Keniston, Gailmarie Pahmeier, and, especially, Chris Coake. And thanks to my graduate and undergraduate students in the courses on American humor writing, place-based creative nonfiction, and western American literary nonfiction that I have taught at UNR in recent years.

Among Reno friends I've received valuable support from Alicia Barber, Pete Barbieri, Roz Bucy, Mike Colpo, Fil Corbitt, Donnie Curtis, Dondo Darue, David Fenimore, Daniel Fergus, Mark Gandolfo, Betty Glass, Torben Hansen, Kent Irwin, Tee Iseminger, Jo Landis, Tony Marek, Ashley Marshall, Eric Rasmussen, James Simmons, Angela Spires, and Jacque Sundstrand. Timely, professional editorial assistance from Laura Ofstad was crucial in bringing this book into port. And thanks to my closest friends, Colin and Monica Robertson and Cheryll and Steve Glotfelty. Special thanks to Cheryll, whose encouragement has been essential to my growth as a writer.

My sincere thanks go to the generous and hardworking folks at *High Country News*, where the "Rants from the Hill" essay series that ultimately led to this book ran online each month from

July 2010 through April 2016. My friend and fellow environmental writer Nick Neely suggested me to *High Country News*, which put the series in motion. The support and assistance of editors Stephanie Paige Ogburn, Jodi Peterson, Paul Larmer, Tay Wiles, Michelle Nijhuis, Diane Sylvain, Cally Carswell, Emily Guerin, and Kate Schimel made it possible for a diverse and enthusiastic readership to spend a few minutes each month with my unusual way of seeing the world. This book would not have been possible without the support of the amazing community of editors, writers, scientists, readers, and activists that has formed around the vitally important work accomplished by *High Country News*.

I'd also like to express my appreciation for the many teachers and readers who have shared my essays. Pieces included in this book have been taught in creative writing or environmental literature courses in at least twenty-five states and have received more than one hundred thousand page views online. Of course, a kitten video posted to YouTube receives more hits than this in a half hour, but it's gratifying to know that so many readers have enjoyed sharing glimpses of our dry slice of life in the high desert. Thanks also to Jessica Ziegler, of Vestor Logic, who constructed my website; please visit at http://michaelbranchwriter.com.

I want to offer very special thanks to George F. Thompson of GFT Publishing. It is impossible to imagine the current vitality of the environmental humanities without the quality books George has brought into the world over the past three decades. George's insightful feedback on an earlier version of this manuscript was crucial in helping to shape it for publication.

I want to express my sincere gratitude to the terrific team at Shambhala/Roost Books, where my recent books have found such a good home. Like the book you now hold, *Raising Wild: Dispatches from a Home in the Wilderness* (2016) and *Rants from the Hill: On Packrats, Bobcats, Wildfires, Curmudgeons, a Drunken Mary*

Kay Lady, and Other Encounters with the Wild in the High Desert (2017) are the work of this team of talented, hardworking folks. Thanks to Breanna Locke (Assistant Editor) and Julia Gaviria for seeing the manuscript down the final stretch, and to Daniel Urban-Brown (Art Director) for making the finished book a thing of beauty that also brings a smile. And thanks to KJ Grow (Sales and Marketing Manager), Claire Kelley (Marketing Manager), and the tireless Jess Townsend (Publicist), whose excellent work has helped my books to find their readers. Most important, I offer my most sincere thanks to Jennifer Urban-Brown (Editor). My ongoing collaboration with Jenn continues to be among the most productive and enjoyable of my career, and I can only hope that folks who mistakenly believe that a writer's relationship with their editor must be adversarial might be as fortunate as I have been in having such a supportive, patient, insightful collaborator in their work.

I am blessed with a family that is exceptionally tolerant of my eccentricities and ambitions, my fierce sense of place, and my idiosyncratic sense of humor. On the other side of the Sierra, thanks to our Central Valley people: O. B. and Deb Hoagland, Sister Kate and Uncle Adam Myers, Troy and Scott Allen, and our brood of cousins—Jenna, Alex, Zev, Ellie, and Quinn. Thanks always to my parents, Stu and Sharon Branch, who have directly or indirectly enabled everything I have accomplished in life.

I often tell our daughters, Hannah and Caroline, that "it takes a family to make a book." The dedication of a book is the sincerest gesture of gratitude available to a writer. It is for this reason that *Raising Wild* was dedicated to my children and *Rants from the Hill* was dedicated to my parents. And so, I have dedicated *How to Cuss in Western* to my wife, Eryn, who is as loving, patient, smart, creative, funny, generous, and encouraging a partner as any desert rat might dream of having. Without her these stories would never have been told, and would never have happened to be told.

Acknowledgments

ABOUT THE AUTHOR

Mⁱᶜʰᵃᵉˡ P. Bʳᵃⁿᶜʰ is Professor of Literature and Environment at the University of Nevada, Reno, where he teaches creative nonfiction, American literature, the literature of humor, environmental studies, and film studies. He has published eight books and more than two hundred essays, articles, and reviews, and his creative nonfiction includes pieces that have received Honorable Mention for the Pushcart Prize and been recognized as Notable Essays in *The Best American Essays* (three times), *The Best American Science and Nature Writing*, and *The Best American Nonrequired Reading* (a humor anthology). He is the recipient of the Ellen Meloy Desert Writers Award, the Nevada Writers Hall of Fame Silver Pen Award, and the Western Literature Association's Manfred Award for Creative Writing and Willa Pilla Award for Humor Writing. His work has appeared in many book-length essay collections and in magazines including *Orion, Ecotone, Utne Reader, Slate, National Parks, Terrain.org, Places, Whole Terrain, Red Rock Review,* and *Sustainable Play.* His books *Raising Wild: Dispatches from a Home in the Wilderness* (2016) and *Rants from the Hill: On Packrats, Bobcats, Wildfires, Curmudgeons, a Drunken Mary Kay Lady, and Other Encounters with the Wild in the High Desert* (2017) were published by Shambhala's Roost Books imprint and are distributed by Penguin Random House.

Mike lives with his wife, Eryn, and daughters, Hannah Virginia and Caroline Emerson, in a passive solar home of their own design at 6,000 feet on a remote hilltop in the high desert of northwestern

Nevada, in the ecotone where the Great Basin Desert and Sierra Nevada Mountains meet. There he writes, plays blues harp, drinks IPA and sour mash, curses at baseball on the radio, cuts stove wood, and walks at least 1,000 miles each year in the surrounding hills, canyons, ridges, arroyos, and playas.

For more information on Mike Branch and his work, please visit his website at http://michaelbranchwriter.com.

ALSO BY MICHAEL P. BRANCH

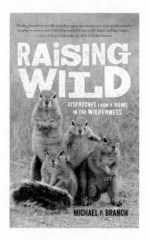

Mᴄʜᴀᴇʟ Bʀᴀɴᴄʜ built his home on a remote hilltop in the Great Basin Desert of northwestern Nevada, a wild and extreme landscape where he lives with his wife and two curious little girls. Moving between pastoral passages on the beauty found in the desert and humorous tales of the humility of being a father, *Raising Wild* offers an intimate portrait of a landscape where mountain lions and ground squirrels can threaten in equal measure. With Branch's distinct lyricism and wit, this exceedingly barren landscape becomes a place resonant with the rattle of snakes, the clatter of pronghorn antelope, and the rustle of juniper trees, a place that is teeming with energy, surprise, and an endless web of connections. Part memoir, part homage to an environment all-to-often dismissed as inhospitable, *Raising Wild* presents an intergenerational approach to nature, family, and the forgotten language of wildness.

WELCOME TO THE LAND OF WILDFIRE, hypothermia, desiccation, and rattlers. The stark and inhospitable high-elevation landscape of Nevada's Great Basin Desert may not be an obvious (or easy) place to settle down, but for self-professed desert rat Michael Branch, it's home. Of course, living in such an unforgiving landscape gives one many things to rant about. Fortunately for us, Branch—humorist, environmentalist, and author of *Raising Wild*—is a prodigious ranter. From bees hiving in the walls of his house to owls trying to eat his daughters' cat—not to mention his eccentric neighbors—adventure, humor, and irreverence abound on Branch's small slice of the world, which he lovingly calls Ranting Hill.